light it up
engaging the introverted student leader

Amma Marfo

People desperately want to know that it's possible to live, act, and work as they are, and introverted leaders who model authenticity will give others freedom to be themselves.

-Adam McHugh

table of contents

preface

"Um, well..."

She seemed to stumble over her words, as she tried to articulate a question that could invalidate my whole premise. I suspected I knew what was coming, but sat quietly and attentive waiting for her to find the words.

"...*are* there introverted student leaders?"

I was going through a round of revisions for an IRB proposal to investigate recruitment strategies for student leadership, with the goal of seeing if certain methods attracted introverted students while others dissuaded them. And the head of our approval committee was visibly baffled by the idea that such a statement was not oxymoronic.

As I fought through multiple rounds of revisions with this committee, defending my choices of instrument and methodology for review, the question surfaced several more times. Each time, I answered as calmly as I could: "Yes, there are- maybe not as you're accustomed to seeing, but it's not only possible, it's more common than you think."

But in my mind, the same thought coursed through my mind: *"This is why I need to do this research."*

Far too many people, be they faculty, staff, workshop facilitators, or even individual students, discount the power of introverts in student involvement and leadership. But as the face of introversion continues to evolve, change, and (oddly enough) get louder, more will need to learn how to foster leadership qualities in introverted students. Grant, Gino and Hoffmann have found in their research that there are some scenarios in which an introverted leader is more effective than the models of leadership and management that we're societally accustomed to.

Many of our notions about the types of students that get involved on our campuses are rooted in Alexander Astin's 1984 *Journal of College Student Development* treatise on involvement, in the first widely documented mention of his Involvement Theory. The final two postulates of the theory are of particular interest to the professionals that work with students to cultivate their involvement, and to help that involvement ascend to leadership:

> *The amount of student learning and personal development associated with any educational program is directly proportional to the quality and quantity of student involvement in that program.*

The effectiveness of any policy or practice is directly related to the capacity of that policy or practice to increase student involvement.

To me, there is an unspoken implication that if a program, policy, or practice isn't aware or nimble enough to respond to the needs of a diverse swath of students (diverse in terms of gender, race, ethnicity, developmental level, sexual orientation, or temperament), then its success will be hindered. While students may succeed despite any obstacles or disparities that this lack of response may cause, we stand to lose more students than we'll keep if we persist in operating in this fashion.

Astin goes on to say that his theory breaks significant ground because it recognizes student time as a finite resource, where previous theories neglected to address that fact:

> According to the theory, the extent to which students can achieve particular developmental goals is a direct function of the time and effort they devote to activities designed to produce these gains [...] The theory of student involvement explicitly acknowledges that the psychic and physical time of students are finite. Thus, educators are competing with other forces in the student's life for a share of that finite time and energy. (emphasis added)

Further, he concedes that "[a]lthough the theory of involvement generally holds that 'more is better,' there are probably limits beyond which increasing involvement ceases to produce desirable results and can even become counterproductive." Why is this important for introverts? I return to an analogy drawn in *The I's Have It* to explain how their energy stores and expenditures differ from their extroverted counterparts:

> Think about the last time you were away from home, phone in hand but in need of a charger. As your device's battery life dwindled, chances are you felt increasingly uncomfortable, perhaps pleading with friends to help you find a charger and an outlet, perhaps preparing for a moment where your device would finally give up, and trying to adapt to the remainder of an evening with no power. That scenario is surprisingly similar to the energy management of an introvert in more challenging [...] situations.

> Like a fully charged cellphone, laptop, or tablet, we all have a finite amount of energy with which we start a day, scenario, or individual interaction. The difference is how the outside world affects that energy store. For extroverts, typical interactions such as conversations with acquaintances and exchanges with strangers serve as, to borrow terminology from the world of Super Mario Brothers, a "power up" button of sorts, allowing them to grow in energy as Mario or Luigi would when they found a star amidst the bricks. They get faster, louder, and more energetic. But for introverts, those interactions are more like Goombas- the side shuffling mushroom enemies of Mario and Luigi. When they encounter

Goombas, they can still function for a time, but they lose some of their shine. They literally grow smaller. And, given enough exposure to the Goombas, they run out of energy completely. So the challenge for introverts, then, is to wear a mask of energy where it would normally actually be de-energizing, to behave as though one had encountered a star instead of a Goomba.

The professionals who work with students to cultivate involvement, and eventually leadership, hold the power (pun not intended, but absolutely recognized) to create programs, policies, and practices that minimally tax participants, that don't unduly drain the aforementioned finite psychic energy that's so essential to a positive and productive experience. The good news is, as knowledge of introversion, combined with additional research on other forms of student development, the viewpoint on this issue is starting to turn in the favor of more introverted students.

What many don't realize is that Astin updated his thoughts on the matter, including what practices "count" as viable involvement opportunities, as he embarked upon research for his theory of spirituality. He elaborated on the connections between the two in a 2012 interview with ACUI's The Bulletin. In it, he recognizes that he previously had not seen certain beneficial practices for spiritual development, as viable parts of the involvement experience.

[Meditation and contemplation and reflection] represents a new form of involvement that we really haven't discussed or utilized in higher education very much. It turned out to be the most powerful type of influence on spiritual growth. If you could pick only one form of involvement, this would be my vote as far as heightening student involvement in the institution and in the educational process.

I wonder if Astin recognizes that his own theory may be to credit/blame when we consider why this more internal form of involvement hasn't previously been encouraged; in his 1984 theory, he dismisses qualifying "words and phrases that are more 'interior' in nature such as value, care for, stress, accentuate and emphasize" for the belief that "involvement implies a behavioral component [...] I am emphasizing that the behavioral aspects, in my judgment, are critical: It is not so much what the individual thinks or feels, but what the individual does, how he or she behaves, that defines and identifies involvement." I imagine now he'd be willing to allow some more active terms to be ascribed to his essential practices: commit oneself to reflection, plunge into solitude, take part in contemplation, etc.

Some critics of the focus on introversion in recent years will rail against the implication that the ability to be contemplative and reflect are not the exclusive purview of introverts. Let me dismiss any potential controversy by wholeheartedly concurring with that sentiment. No behavior is outside the bounds of any temperament; this is a constant refrain in my research, scholarship, and presentation on this topic. However, from a neurological standpoint, these activities are more energizing for introverts than they are for extroverts:

There are two chemicals in the brain that control our response to stimuli: dopamine and acetylcholine. The former is responsible for the "fight or flight" response: it gets our hearts racing, blood pumping faster, and provides the rush of energy needed to flee the threat at hand. If it were powering a car, it'd be most like the turbo boost available on some sports cars.

The latter is responsible for calming us down and enabling our ability to focus deeply and concentrate. It also is responsible for our partial paralysis and REM sleep each night. If dopamine powers the turbo boost, acetylcholine functions much like cruise control. All humans have some level of both dopamine and acetylcholine coursing through their brains. However, recent research has determined that the brains of those who differ in temperament also differ in the levels of these hormones and the dominant pathways on which these hormones travel. If you guessed that extroverts have more dopamine and that introverts have more acetylcholine...bingo. You nailed it. Here are a few reasons why these hormonal differences are important:

Introverts are chemically equipped to concentrate. Acetylcholine, as I mentioned previously, is the hormone that allows deep concentration. This explains the introverted tendency to learn a great deal about areas of interest with relative ease. But from an office standpoint, it works against us for a key element to student affairs:

interruption. Variety in a workday keeps things interesting, as do unanticipated challenges that arise each day, courtesy of our students. But after these impromptu meetings, student crises, or last-minute errands, introverts have a harder time returning to their regularly scheduled programming.

The neural pathway on which acetylcholine travels is longer than the one on which dopamine travels. This makes it harder to get started again once it is preempted by a situation that creates a flow of dopamine. A chemical aversion to interruption can be even more difficult for introverts who work in cubicles or as a part of open-office plans. A lack of a barrier to interruptions can keep them operating at a suboptimal rate.

Acetylcholine releases more delicate stimulation than dopamine. The stimulation that acetylcholine does provide is a more subdued form of energy than that which dopamine stimulates. It can easily be fueled by quiet conversation, by the noises of nature, or an easygoing conversation with a close friend. This form of stimulation is simply not enough to satisfy the dopamine-fueled brains of most extroverts, who need the greater rush of more animated exchanges and the constant drone of a TV or radio in the background. Interestingly enough, this pattern switches when it's time to drift off to sleep; introverts may like music or a white noise machine to drown out the whirring of their own thoughts, but too much noise or stimulation keeps some extroverts from sleeping.

This revision incorporates reflection practices that tend to come naturally to introverts; as such, students who we previously would have labeled disengaged or uninvolved are now considered viable candidates for leadership. However, our practices in five major areas of student involvement and leadership (recruitment, selection and training, advising and supervision, evaluation and assessment, and rewards and recognition) have remained similarly outdated when engaging this population of students. And with recent statistics indicating that between 1/3 and 1/2 of the population identifies as introverted*, it's a large swath of the college-attending public that is being ignored without attention to these long-standing practices.

But Astin's more recent research implies that this can be fixed, if higher-level decision makers will recognize the value of adapting to this need. He recommends "think[ing] about creative ways to give students to engage in reflection and meditation. Have designated spaces in the unions where students can do this that are not necessarily religious in nature- just quiet places." Further, he suggests encouraging all students to find the value in these practices, challenging them to create space to answer essential contemplative questions about their experience. "Why are you in school? What do you want to accomplish with your life? Who are you? What kind of person are you?" We often allow students to shy away from addressing these queries, agreeing with their assessment that they have no right answer, or are hard to know when you're young. However, this is a poor excuse to avoid them; "[t]hese are the big questions that every student has to confront. Very often, we can go through undergraduate work and never put any thought into it when really these are fundamental questions."

My primary recommendation for working with all student leaders: create space for these questions to be addressed. All students will benefit from it, but the introverts will thrive in particular because they were built to consider these questions, and live their lives in their context. As we move through the five stages of the student involvement and leadership experience, many of my recommendations for programmatic changes and considerations will be predicated on the idea that contemplation and reflection are essential to the station of leader. While you may not agree with, or even be able to implement, the suggestions that I share in these pages, I hope you'll consider their impact- not just on your introverted students, but any student seeking to find success on your campus.

introduction

Before we dive into the strategies and systems that can help introverts (and extroverts alike!) get the most out of their student leadership and involvement experience, I want to ensure that we are on the same page as far as what introversion is, and what it isn't. At the time of publication of this book, introversion is both highly visible and highly misunderstood. It is recognized as a more common trait than ever before.

I want to provide an illustration to demonstrate what many think about introversion versus what it actually is. And, true to form, I'd like to use a movie to do it: 1993's dramatization of the All-American Women's Baseball League, *A League of their Own*.

In *A League of their Own*, there was a character named Marla Hooch who I'm convinced serves as the archetype for introversion in most people's minds. She spoke little, had relatively few close relationships (with her father, and later her husband Nelson), but was outstanding at what she had chosen to focus on for so many years. I think you'd agree that there are relatively few people in our lives like Marla; in fact, introversion is only proving to be more and more common and is shown to be valuable at the helm of successful companies like LinkedIn, Apple, and Campbell's Soup. And yet, it still evokes images of trembling before parties or networking events, declining to speak up at meetings or in front of groups, or avoiding it altogether and taking on the role of recluse.

Sometimes a good way to focus on what something is, can be to focus on what it isn't. To that end, I want to focus on busting some myths associated with introversion (and for that matter, its counterpart in extroversion).

Introverts don't like people. This is perhaps the most pervasive myth haunting introverts. In reality, I know as many extroverts that don't care for people, as I do introverts. Their seeming dislike, however, is rooted in different things. While introverts don't, by nature, gain energy from social situations, that doesn't mean that they don't care to be around people. In fact, when in relationships with people they trust and care about, introverts are the most caring and even energetic people you may meet. They simply recognize that social situations don't give them energy in the same way that it does for extroverts. Introverts require time and considerable energy to warm up to people- when allotted that time, and when around the right people, they can flourish.

As a follow-up, I want to bust the myth that temperament (both extroversion and introversion) are grounded in social factors. Adam Grant says it best when he too busts myths about introversion:

If you're an introvert, you're more prone to being overstimulated by intense or prolonged social interaction—and at that point, reflecting on your thoughts and feelings can help you recharge. But introversion-extraversion is about more than just social interaction. Extraverts crave stimulating activities like skydiving and stimulating beverages sold at Starbucks. Introverts are more likely to retreat to a quiet place, but they're very happy to bring someone else with them.

That form of stimulation that energizes extroverts and drains introverts could be the result of many things- social interaction, temperature, even caffeine or hunger!

Introverts are shy. Closely related to the previous myth, many people (introverts included, at times!) are of the belief that introversion and shyness are one and the same. Not so. Susan Cain puts it best in her book *Quiet: The Power of Introverts in a World That Can't Stop Talking* when she notes that introversion is a preference toward ideas, while shyness is a fear of social situations. The former is tiring, while the latter is painful. It's also worth noting that while shyness refers to social situations, introversion comes into play with any form of excessive stimulation (including temperature, pain, or even hunger).

Introverts are quiet. Is this a myth? Is this true? To quote one of my favorite professors, "it depends." Introverts who are shy, will be prone to long periods of quiet. But as we just learned, this quiet is symptomatic of shyness, not introversion. Social introverts (yep, that's a thing!) and introverts in situations that draw less energy from them are not as quiet. In fact, they may appear to "extrovert" (more on that later) better than most. But look closely- they may maintain that level of energy for a shorter period than others. Some introverts are quiet, but so are some shy extroverts (yep, also a thing). Look deeper before assigning this label.

Introverts can't lead. In early research on introverted student leaders, I met some resistance from colleagues who insisted that such a term was an oxymoron. But as we dug deeper and talked to students in leadership positions, we learned it was far more common than most would imagine. Society is starting to recognize this fact, as leaders like Bill Gates, Warren Buffet, LinkedIn's Jeff Weiner and even President Obama are gaining attention for the leadership they provide while honoring their introverted tendencies. Introverts may not always appear at the front of a room with boundless energy, but they can have influence when in the right spaces and supported by good people. In fact, Grant, Gino and Hoffman found that in some cases, introverts can be better leaders than their extroverted counterparts!* So if you're looking to bring someone into power, don't overlook introverts! And introverts, if you're nervous about going for it- take a chance. You could be great!

Introversion is cultural. Introversion isn't the dominant culture in the United States; that said, it is more common in different cultures. Many Asian cultures revere qualities associated with introversion, for example and with that comes more acceptance in those countries. However, that doesn't mean that all Asians are introverted, any more than all Americans are extroverted. Introversion and extroversion exists in varying levels of abundance around the world. This myth is a good one to remember when traveling, so as to calibrate your behavior based on how the culture behaves, but is not to be wielded as a means to generalize about people.

Introverts and extroverts can't get along. With differences in lifestyle, social preference, and energy, it may seem as though a harmonious union between these two types. Introversion researcher (and extrovert!) Jennifer Kahnweiler believes differently. In her book *Genius of Opposites*, she dedicates her pages to demonstrating how introverts and extroverts are the perfect business partners. In her mind,

> The sooner that introverts and extroverts learn about each other's different languages, the quicker they can get to results. We would together in offices, on conference calls, and through text messages. Yet it often feels like we introverts and extroverts are speaking entirely different languages. We need to learn how to glide seamlessly in and out of these conversations with as little stress as possible. Being able to do this not only gets results but is also personally gratifying.

For my part, one of my best friends is an extrovert, and he's wonderful at encouraging me to think bigger on projects when I need ideas. Conversely, when those ideas need to be focused and narrowed down, I really excel. Whatever type you lean toward (keeping in mind always that everyone has elements of both!), the odds are good that having a friend or significant other in the opposite camp can make you stronger and more well-rounded.

Introversion can be faked. I hear all the time that introverts feel as though they have to "fake" extroversion in some situations. It always bothers me when I hear someone "faked extroversion" to get through a big speech or a long party. Conversely, friends of mine who have to spend more time alone or have to sit quietly will sometimes claim they're "faking" introversion. But I don't see it that way.

In my mind, behaviors aren't introverted or extroverted, people are. And no behavior is outside of the bounds of anyone's ability. But, activities like parties or other social situations are easier for extroverts because those situations give them energy. Similarly, being alone and reflection tend to be easier for introverts because they get a charge in those moments. So no one ever "fakes" one temperament or another; rather, you give off the appearance that a less energizing activity is easy.

Introversion can be "fixed." This is actually a relatively new myth to me, that I saw in the comments of a TED talk about introversion. One rather vocal commenter claimed to have "learned" to not be introverted anymore, and that those who still owned the title simply weren't trying hard enough.

Believe it or not, there may be something to this one. Not much, but some.

As I mentioned before, introversion isn't about not being able to do "extroverted things," but rather being able to convey that these things are easy. Indeed, some elements of life that can challenge introverts (like public speaking, or breaking into new groups of people) can be made easy when we learn the best way to do them for ourselves without them draining our energy. This has been true for me with public speaking- anything that we're used to, gets easier. And yet. The need, the natural tendency, the physiological need to turn inward in order to get our energy back...never goes away. Even the most comfortable social situations won't give you energy, they'll simply deplete it at a slower rate. So introverts, you can "train" to operate out in the world, but your introverted ways will never go away. Spend the time learning how to make the world work for you, and you'll shine just as brightly- albeit differently- as your extroverted counterparts.

I want to dedicate this book to changing the image that comes to mind when you think about an involved introvert. It shouldn't look like *A League of their Own*'s Marla Hooch anymore, struggling painfully to endure a baseball season by hiding behind her hair. Instead, I want you to think about her teammate Dottie Hinson. As most people do when considering what introversion look like, you may have discounted her introversion. But look a little closer: she absolutely fits the bill. Dottie took the time to get to know people, had a few close relationships, and did her job well (including being an inspiration for the team) without much fanfare. Even when the spotlight was turned her way, she shied away from it or sought to turn it toward other people. All of these, and not Marla's timid shyness, are realistic hallmarks of introverts in control of their style. Seek to inspire a legion of Dotties, able to manage their energy and shine bright on our campuses and in our organizations. The pages ahead will show you how.

chapter 1

A LETTER TO THE EXTROVERTED READER

Hi there, and welcome! I can't tell you how glad I am to see you.

A part of me feels compelled to apologize. I can't help but feel like the rise of the introvert has left extroverts feeling vilified, cast wrongly as brash screamers incapable of listening or thinking about their actions. I don't believe that, and truly never have. In fact, I have been public about the degree to which extroverts are needed and valuable.

Do I wish to champion the cause of introverts? Absolutely. I wouldn't be so reverent of the work that Susan Cain has done, or devote my time to writing my own book on the subject, if I didn't think that their nature didn't need to be highlighted. However, I think the understanding of the introvert shouldn't need to be paired with the demonization of the extrovert. To crack a joke often used in other circles, "Some of my best friends are extroverts!"

So know that even though we are different, and even though we may have a hard time understanding each other, I want to sing the praises of the extroverted. I salute you. Here are a few reasons why:

Extroverts are includers. So many horror stories around introversion are centered around a more extroverted individual trying to get him to do something they're not always comfortable with. Examples include going to parties where he may not know someone, pulling her out on a dance floor, or encouraging them to stay the extra hour at a networking event when she's already tired.

However, think about what that really means. It's not the sordid plot of someone trying to pry a friend from his or her comfort zone. Rather, it's a natural tendency to want to create connections between people. Those energized by outward stimulation like to gather their friends and family around them, and to be pushed into a raucous situation means they appreciate and want your company. So feel uncomfortable if you must, but also feel loved!

Extroverts prompt action. I can't speak for all introverts, but I will say that decision making and determining a course of action takes me a long time. As a result of that, new initiatives or changes to old ones are hard for me to make. Not because I can't make the change, but I'm insistent upon having all the details in place before I get them executed.

The beauty of extroverts in a world that moves as quickly as ours is that they move at a similar speed. They can make a decision and commit to all it involves fairly quickly. And that sort of quick decisiveness is something I really value in my more extroverted counterparts.

Extroverts can be quiet too! When I stopped by my director's office yesterday, he happened to be talking about introversion and extroversion with a pair of our students. He asked me to guess if one of them was introverted and extroverted (sometimes it gets to be like a party trick, as he is an extrovert who doesn't fully understand the nuances of either type), and I ended up being correct. The other student in the office mentioned that he was extroverted, but was also quiet.

I appreciated him for saying this, because we sometimes forget. Just like not all introverts are not shy or quiet, not all extroverts are loud and rambunctious. Introversion and extroversion live on opposite sides of a spectrum, not opposing sides of a coin. There is grey all over the place, and we all live in it.

I'm writing this book as a means to support introverted students, a competency that none of us, irrespective of temperament, are adequately trained in. As you work through this book, you'll notice that many of the strategies listed evoke a feeling of, "Well, that works for me too!"

That's the idea.

None of these strategies, notes, or recommendations are to elevate one population at the expense of the other. Rather, they're designed to incorporate practices that will create a more welcoming and comfortable environment for those who need an adjustment. I hope when you find something new that strikes a chord, you'll not only seek to build that into your professional practices, but also create space for it in your own routine! And when you do, I hope you'll head to ammamarfo.com/lightitupbook and let me know how it goes- successes, struggles, and everything in between.

INsights: Five Things You Can Do to Start Capacity-Building Relationships with Introverts Today

1.   Pay close attention to the students who linger by booths or at information sessions- these are potentially engaged leaders, even if they don't speak up right away. Take an interest in who they are- a personal connection will entice them to get involved. (Recruitment)

2.   How densely packed are your training sessions? If you're not building in breaks, seriously consider creating space for more than just the standard biological needs- let information sink in, and psychological batteries recharge. (Selection and Training)

3.   Vary contribution methods when you advise-meetings can feature spoken input, but also written or drawn contributions. Additionally, be vocal about the option to follow up after meetings with thoughts that may have arrived later than expected. (Advising and Supervision)

4.   If evaluations happen with a set of questions, provide those questions ahead of time. The ability to ponder and prepare will enrich the quality of responses you receive. (Evaluation and Assessment)

5.   If your award nomination process features submissions, share the nomination letters or blurbs with those who are up for recognition. This additional artifact of their impact will empower in a far greater way than you might imagine. (Recognition and Rewards)

Thanks so much for "being here," seriously. I hope you enjoy!

chapter 2

A LETTER TO THE INTROVERTED READER

Hi there, and welcome. You're among friends.

Our profile is rising, and it's an exciting time! Things about yourself you've had a hard time articulating- why your clearest thoughts come after a conversation rather than during, why multi-day training and retreats has you so much more drained than your peers, why icebreakers send your eyes all the way back- are finally out in the open, and we stand a better chance of being understood than we ever have. What a time to be alive!

With that said, you may still need this book.

"But if I know myself well enough to operate as an introvert," you may be wondering, "why do I need to learn how to work with introverted students?"

To answer that, I'll take you back a few years to our interviews for orientation leader positions. I sat in on scores of interviews, with applicants spanning all walks of life and types of involvement on campus. Even knowing how I am in interviews and even as I was conducting research for *The I's Have It* on how introverts could excel in interviews...I found myself placing higher value and competence on the interviews of the students for whom it came naturally. The ones who had polished answers that came easily, the ones for whom interviewing was an energizing process. You'll note as you continue reading: I don't believe that any skill is the province of one type over the other; rather, they look different in each type based on how much ease or effort is required to do them well.

It goes without saying that many extroverts are affirmed when the pursue leadership roles- they seem predestined for all the competencies that it requires, somehow. But without realizing it, many introverts have bought into the hype that extroverts are designed to be leaders too. Further, the training we receive in graduate programs and professional development opportunities reinforces ideas about engagement and involvement that reinforce what Susan Cain calls "the extrovert ideal." No matter how much rest you need after a retreat, or no matter how much you may value your quiet time in the early mornings or late evenings, you may still unconsciously lean toward elevating students for whom the present structure of leadership is effortless. I'm here to not only challenge that assumption, but equip you with the tools to bring this out in students whose stories probably resemble yours pretty closely. If we seek to challenge students in order to help them find their greatest and most effective selves, this means placing them in situations that, while not easy, are rewarding. Involvement and leadership can fall under that umbrella.

As an introvert who relates with the plight of the students you're seeking to reach, you have advantages in this fight to create confident and skilled introverted student leaders. Your natural propensity for listening will help students as they seek affirmation and understanding in new pursuits. Your understanding of what introverts' quirks may look like can help you advocate for them in scenarios where colleagues and fellow students are still unsure. And your innate tendency to think before acting will help you in crafting activities, experiences, and opportunities for introverts to shine. You can do this, and your introverted students need you to. I'll close this letter with a few small tips that will get you started. Some of these may be things you're already doing, some you may want to try as you work your way through the book. In either case, please know that you're an invaluable resource for introverted students who are looking to make their mark. I can't wait to hear more about how you'll do that, and urge you to share with me how you do. Please reach out to me at ammamarfo.com/lightitupbook and keep me posted!

INsights: Five Things You Can Do to Start Capacity-Building Relationships with Introverts Today

1.   Seek to build relationships with students who show quiet interest. Think about the ones who come to meetings and appear engaged, but may not always speak up in

conversations or stay after for mingling. Take note of their interests and style of interacting, and establish a rapport. (Recruitment)

2.   In scenarios where you have say over students that get selected for roles, draw attention to alternate interpretations of common introvert behaviors, such as "defensive" posture or prolonged quiet before responses. In a vacuum, assumptions can be made; it is only with insight that we can interpret these unconscious cues differently. (Selection)

3.   Be a custodian of quiet space for students who may need it for reflection. Provide it in your office when possible, and advertise its availability and advocate for its use around and off campus. (Advising/Supervision)

4.   When it comes time to encapsulate experiences, be mindful of the idea that impact and learning is hard to verbalize. Provide opportunities for students to reflect along the way, and allow these artifacts or experiences to supplement their evaluation experience. (Assessment/ Evaluation)

5.   Be the advocate for quiet and consistent recognition. A small "thank you" or "good job" goes a long way, as I'm sure you've experience. Model the importance of these quieter expressions of gratitude and excellence by acting on them in the moment. (Recognition and Rewards)

INTERLUDE: Considering the Shy Extrovert
by Curtis Tarver

I have spoken often about the two dimensions of temperament- introversion/extroversion as well as shy/outgoing, and provided the case of the ongoing introvert. However, its opposite- the shy extrovert- is talked about less often. So I enlisted Curtis to share his take on the phenomenon, demystifying it for those who have trouble conceiving of such a thing.

Knowing about your temperament is all about being aware of where you get your energy, but simply knowing that doesn't mean it's always easy to access. The concept of an introvert who doesn't have adequate time apart from others to recharge is pretty easy to imagine. But there's another side to that coin: the shy extrovert.

For some less versed in introversion and extroversion, the term may seem oxymoronic. Shyness is often associated with - and sometimes incorrectly labeled as - introversion, making it seem to run counter to the concept of extroversion. While introversion and extroversion denote one's chief energy source, the shy-outgoing scale is more about the comfort or ease with which one engages with others. In the case of a shy extrovert, there may be opportunities to engage in way that would be fulfilling, but seizing such opportunities proves difficult.

To be fair, I'd probably just as readily be classified an ambivert. I sit just a few clicks off center in the extroverted direction - type does, after all, exist along a continuum - but I've rarely questioned my energy source. Still, in social situations, I don't always find it easy to tap into. At a gathering where I only know a few people, I can find myself on the fringe of a conversation or two. In situations where I know no one, I can find it difficult to engage at all, leading to an interesting quandary: I can leave such an event feeling drained, not from the social interaction as an introvert may, but from the lack of it, despite it being readily available. There are times, for example, when a common cause but not necessarily common people brings me into a situation, and as much as I may want to strike up a conversation with the person I'm standing next to, it's difficult to do. I also find that my shy extroversion isn't always social situation-specific. It may take on the form of, "I'd love to get out and meet the neighbors, but…"

I've found that I thrive in situations with planned interaction. While ice breakers and small talk with starters may be hell on introverts, they are a welcome foot in the door for a shy extrovert. Social situations with structure make for chances to connect with others without having to direct traffic to oneself. I, in turn, have found that I enjoy creating spaces for being social with structure, having served as a social chair and worked in campus programming. I find that I'm comfortable in the spotlight, but I don't seek it. In fact, I'm often more comfortable on the stage than striking up a small conversation.

A corollary to the planned interaction is the all-important introduction. A shy extrovert is likely to stick to those who are familiar; an introduction provides the initial connection necessary to grow one's network and in turn one's energy source. As a friend or colleague in such a setting, it may also serve to detach them from their comfort zone, which may well be you. While a shy extrovert is less likely to be a social butterfly, expanding their available go-tos should set them up for success.

chapter 3

RECRUITMENT

I still remember the email that appeared in my inbox, in late July of 2004.

It was the then-current president of the Student Alumni Association (SAA), Rosie, thanking me for showing interest in the organization at an information session during freshman orientation a few weeks prior. She also complimented the online handle I used for my email (theladyram2008), noting it as a sign that the organization was going to be a great fit for me.

I also remember the moment when my orientation leader, Katie, pulled me aside on the first day of orientation to let me know that she was also a part of the Student Entertainment Committee (SEC), and she thought I'd fit in great with the group. She asked me to promise her that I'd apply, and answered my questions about how they worked and what I could do.

It may go without saying that these interactions are memorable because of the impact that they had on my course of involvement in college. But just so we're clear, the two organizations that I dedicated my full college career to are the ones listed above. I count their members among some of my dearest friends to this day (including both Rosie and Katie), and my return to New England in 2012 was executed in part to be closer to the people that made these experiences so rewarding.

I compare the feelings of warmth, acceptance, and security that came from these small moments, to the overwhelming and panicky feeling that I got from other measures designed to encourage students to get involved on campus. First Night, the massive involvement fair that takes over the Union and its surrounding areas, engulfed me with its crush of students and loud noises. And lest it be believed that the feelings came from being new, I felt that way every year, even when I was recruited to stand on the other side of the table to welcome new students in subsequent years.

How many of us trust the process of student recruitment to a one-off dazzling display, designed to "pull students in" with engaging activities and other diversions to hold their attention? While the energy is important to show students that their campus is a vibrant place where there are things to do, this method could also backfire, leading more introverted students to feel that there aren't spaces "for them." Particularly because these events happen so early (see the title "First Night"), they may not yet have learned to manage their energy in their newly adopted space. By the time their equilibrium has been ascertained, and they're ready to incorporate new elements of the college experience into their cultivated routine, who's available to help them ease into the process?

In Astin's seminal paper outlining his theory of student involvement, he outlines the "Resource Theory" of pedagogy (which, despite its terminology, does extend to student services). He writes, "the resource theory maintains that if adequate resources are brought together in one place, student learning and development will occur." It's easy to see where campus traditions like new student orientation and involvement fairs fit the bill of this theory. However, it does have its limitations, and Astin cautions against those too. He cautions against using a critical mass of quantity as the lone tool in one's arsenal to get students involved. However, "the [...] problem with this approach is its focus on mere accumulation of resources with little attention given to the use or deployment of such resources."

As I speak to introverted students about their experiences on campus, they repeatedly cite the importance of the small moments with other students and staff members as the ones that had the most impact on their involvement experience. Nicole Onofreo, a current graduate student at The University of South Florida and former student intern at Emmanuel College, conducted an interview with introverted students to learn more about the effectiveness of student involvement recruitment practices. She spoke to students in varying organizations, involved in a variety of activities and at various levels. A common thread she found was the significance and gravity that personal interactions held in the decision to join an organization or partake in an activity:

> *"I remember the exact conversation. I was in the bathroom during my Italian class and I saw the president at the time in the bathroom. I told her that I was really interested in becoming involved in OUTspoken and she offered me the [secretary] position on the spot. Then I remember her sitting me down in February the next semester and telling me that she was going to step down and wanted me to be President because I would give the organization the attention it needed."*

> *"The first position I had was being a part of the 1804 Society, which my First-Year Seminar professor nominated me for. I was honored by her nomination and thought I would apply but did not expect to be a part of the program. After that, I was also asked to be a coordinator for the E-List Committee on campus, and asked to be a supervisor of the [...] Community Center on campus. Essentially, I have found out about all of my involvement through individuals telling me about opportunities."*

Astin does allude to the perceived effectiveness of such an approach in his examination of the "individualized (eclectic) theory":

> It emphasizes, for instance, the Importance to the student of advising and counseling and of independent study. The philosophy underlying most

student personnel work (guidance, counseling, selective placement, and student support services) implicitly incorporates the individualized or eclectic theory of student development.

While Astin does concede that this isn't always a tenable goal due to size of a student body and an infinite number of ways students may need to be approached, he does identify it as the method best geared toward those working with students outside the classroom. Additionally, because student affairs professionals already work with students in a more individualized manner than most faculty do, they have the tools to operationalize this strategy "at the ready," so to speak.

It is worth noting, however, in light of the question posed "are there introverted student leaders?", that these positions of involvement or leadership should be looked at with an eye on students with a variety of temperaments being able to succeed within them. It is not to say that introverted students require accommodation or coddling of any kind; rather, I mean to examine the time commitment and scope of duties for their ability to be introvert-friendly. Onofreo notes in her study, "introverted students felt that the involvement positions they were involved in were designed for students with extroverted personalities, potentially leading to less interest from introverted students. When introverted students were asked if their personalities and their assigned duties 'matched' their personality types, every interviewee disagreed."

Although I agree with Onofreo about the setup of many student leadership expectations and think there is room for adaptation in these expectations, I also fervently believe that it is a worthwhile endeavor to push students beyond where they're comfortable. Most students recognize that this will happen and report for duty regardless:

> "A lot of my involvement journey is me pushing myself out of my comfort zone. A lot of my involvement involves talking to people, sometimes-large groups of people. Or even organizing events and attending them. Or disciplinary actions. Which takes a lot of energy from me."

> "I loved being an [Orientation Leader]- however, I often found that I had to take breaks during the day even for a few minutes to be alone and recharge. Whether it was going to the bathroom during a meal or just enjoying the quiet while the students were in session, I learned to adapt and recharge when need be."

The second testimonial demonstrates that students are finding these coping mechanisms on their own, and are finding ways to succeed despite expectations of more ease in these roles (again, the question is not if introverts can serve in these roles, but with what level of ease these competencies are demonstrated). But if we truly believe that one strength of Astin's student involvement theory is to acknowledge that students' psychic and physical time are limited, then we too must care for students during this key transition point in their college career. As such, I will conclude with some actions you can take to cultivate and nurture an "introvert-friendly" recruitment culture on your campus.

Don't dispense with the involvement fair. This may seem counterintuitive to my prior pages, and in some ways I suppose it is. As a professional who has played a significant role in the organization and presentation of these events on campuses for nearly ten years, I am often personally conflicted about their utility. But ultimately, I believe that they do hold some value. First and foremost, there is the simple fact that some students (introverted and extroverted) do benefit from them from an involvement standpoint. There are students who do pull energy from the social buzzing and wide landscape of opportunities spread spatially before them, and it would be as irresponsible to deny them that chance to thrive in that human-derived energy, as it is to force such a structure upon those that don't.

Further, a challenge issued to student groups to represent themselves with more than just a signup sheet and members in T-shirts provides an exercise in creativity that I truly enjoy presenting to students. It is a joy to see them stretch to meet the expectations we set, giving booth visitors the chance to participate in the goals of their organization, if only for a few minutes.

Additionally, there is a preparatory element to the continued presence of involvement fairs on our campuses. They also represent a type of challenge that all students will need to be able to operate in beyond our walls. Trade expos, large scale career fairs, academic and professional conferences-regardless of temperament, all students hold the potential to have to operate successfully in those spaces. As I do not advocate using temperament as a crutch or excuse to decline opportunities, I do believe there is instructive value in helping students navigate these spaces successfully. To that end, I'd be sure to provide guides to students (both "exhibiting" and attending) on where booths/displays are located, so they can navigate this potentially overwhelming and draining experience effectively.

Consider smaller, targeted follow-up opportunities. As I mentioned previously, there are some who may not be prepared to make their involvement decisions right away. Once classes begin and routines are eased into, students may return to the idea of getting involved and want to seek out organizations to explore. Is it possible to create opportunities for segments of groups (club sports, fraternal/ sororal organizations, service groups, academic clubs) to gather again and share current projects with students? These smaller "mini-fairs" allow students to attend based on their desire to pursue a certain course of involvement without the inundation of additional options they won't take. And for the students representing their organizations, it provides an instructive opportunity to keep them in a "growth mindset." We've often seen groups become insular after traditional "intake" periods; this need to continue outreach can mitigate this instinct.

Examine and articulate the benefits and requirements of involvement. I vividly recall a friend of mine from college who resisted applying for a position on our programming board because she knew members attended a conference each year, and she thought she'd be required to fly there, something she'd never done before. She participated as a general member for a full year without knowing that this trip wasn't required. How many students self-opt out of experiences they'd thrive in, because of their belief of what's required?

As you introduce applications for coveted leadership positions of your own design, **be as open as possible about what the role requires.** Pay close attention to issues of time commitment, connection to academic requirements, and specific duties. As an example, I've seen many students of varying temperaments decline student government roles because they fear public speaking- something that isn't required in all roles but can appear to be. Further, examine the duties and requirements of roles you're recruiting for and see if it is a position that many types of students could succeed in. What duties are truly required, and which ones are just nice to have? Are the time commitments cited required, or can they be flexible if a student needs more time to ease in or recharge in the process?

Encourage faculty and staff outreach. As a few testimonials indicated, the trust of a professor or staff member in a student's ability can push them to reach for opportunities they may not have previously considered. This is a small way to individualize a student's experience, even if classroom or organizational involvement can't always be customized. Do you have a student in a class that has shown an exceptional ability to explain concepts or feel others in a group feel welcome? Send them a quick note or start a quick conversation around the time of orientation leader or tour guide applications. Has a student shown keen interest in a topic in an introductory course? Encourage their application for an executive board role in the organization's student group. And if you happen to oversee selection (which we'll get into shortly) for a given leadership role, reach out to faculty and staff to formally nominate individuals, then share these nominations with students. It is amazing how powerful this recognition of potential can be for a student on the fence about applying or joining.

Encourage peer outreach and mentorship. As an earlier testimony can attest, the trust and confidence of a classmate or friend can galvanize an individual who may not otherwise have been moved to apply or participate alone. While faculty and staff recognition is helpful and worthwhile, peer outreach can be as powerful, if not more powerful, because of the implicit social acceptance it signifies. Work with current student leaders on identifying qualities in their peers that could benefit the legacy of their chosen organization, and help them seek out ways to draw high-potential peers into the organization (e.g. shadowing, "board member for a day," behind-the-scenes access to a meeting or event). With an eye on the legacy of their organization, this could simplify the transition process for all and ensure the longevity of strong groups.

We cannot develop a diverse slate of involved students and student leaders, without ensuring that their path to us is as equitable as it can be. Seek to engage, not overwhelm, the students that may be more tentative to join the ranks- trust me, they want to, but may need a different path in. Don't be afraid to provide it, they'll do some wonderful things for you!

INsights: 5 Ways to Recruit Introverts to Involvement and Leadership Opportunities Today

1. **If you see something, say something.** Take a moment to encourage students who show potential to become part of your program. Be it through an email, a short in-person conversation, or a note slipped in a locker or under a door, the personal touch counts.
2. **Coach student leaders and other involved students to do the same.** As the quoted students share, their potential being seen by other students meant enough to them to push them past apprehensions and worries.
3. **Create multiple outreach opportunities.** In addition to your standard moments of exposure in orientation presentations, tours, and involvement fairs, consider offering additional smaller opportunities for students to find out about the involvement options on campus.
4. **Make the requirements crystal clear.** What does involvement or leadership need from individuals wishing to get involved? Move past vague platitudes like "leadership skills" and "meeting people" to estimated time commitments and required travel or showcase opportunities.
5. **Highlight a diverse slate of involved leaders.** When advertising involvement initiatives, allow others to see themselves in the role by letting multiple types of leaders and involved students speak about their time in the role, what they've enjoyed, and what it's given them.

Next, we'll be exploring how to choose the best candidates for your coveted positions, as well as how to bring them onboard the organization in a manner that fits their temperament and needs.

INTERLUDE: An Extrovert's Take on Introversion
by Jeff Parker

So many of our rituals and habits are catered toward extraverts. Weddings, going away parties, work outings, concerts, etc... it seems as if everything we do in our lives is determined by how many people we can cram into one particular spot. Even in the virtual world, our status is measured by how many friends we have, likes or retweets we get, and comments people post.

In the student affairs world, we do the same thing. Let's say you spend a few thousand dollars to bring a speaker in to present on a given topic. You advertise for months, create all sorts of social media buzz, and exert so much energy getting the word out. Only a dozen student show up, but the ones that do all get some sort of earth-shattering result out of attending. In the vast majority of circles, that is a failure because only a dozen people showed up. What those dozen students got out of attending is often buried beneath the notion that the money was wasted. This is what we do when we interact with introverts. We tell them that they are a failure because they don't know everyone on their floor, join several organizations, or immerse themselves in everything a university has to offer. For introverts, breadth is not important; depth is. Yet in our residence halls, if a student doesn't have his/her door open every waking moment, that student is a recluse. If he/she can't make it to the athletic event, comedian, RA program, AND their study group, then he/she is "not involved enough" at the university. We spend more time telling students what they should be interested in instead of asking what they are getting meaning out of. Extraverts love bouncing from event to event, making their appearances, being seen, and adding things to their list of titles at the end of their email signatures (we've all seen it). Introverts find meaning in other ways, and focus on the depth of their interactions and their experiences. Then we tell them they're not doing "enough."

What frustrates me the most about peoples' views of introversion is the notion that introverts don't like people and want to be alone. All the time. Heaven forbid if an introvert is in the vicinity of another human being, their head might explode. Introverts don't watch the movie Cast Away and think that's a new career goal. Introverts like people too! In fact, they may like people more than us extraverts do (gasp!). While we're off putting on a show and dazzling groups of people en masse, introverts are having a one on one interaction, getting to know someone on a deeper level. They're developing a meaningful relationship, investing in that person's life, and getting energized by that connection they are making. And that moment is more real, valuable, and inspiring than introverts are given credit for.

I think the best way may be to look at each department, division, or campus as a team and cater to the strengths that each of us possess. We don't expect our residence life departments to go on the road and recruit high school students. We don't expect admissions to respond to on call crises in the residence halls. We don't expect our student activities department to administer sanctions for students nor do we expect our student conduct department to host our week of welcome or homecoming events. Each department has their own focuses, strengths, and ideas for how to impact the students' experience. In general, students affairs does a good job recognizing that and partnering with each other to make smart and sound collaborative endeavors. Why don't we take this notion to heart at the micro level and understand that everyone has different strengths, and we should cater to those. We evaluate positions that are on the same level the same way. If there are 5 RDs, they are going to be evaluated by the same forms in the same way. What if one RD is exceptional with operations and one with developing cohesion amongst the RAs? What if one is exceptional in programming and another in facility management? What if one goes to every RA program after hours and another constantly has students in his/her office throughout the work day? This is just one area, but every department faces the same struggle. Everyone does things in a different way, yet we are measured (often against each other) by the same means. But who determines which is the best way? I am one to say that success happens in a variety of ways and can look different for everyone. You can have two people with completely different strategies, ideas, and how they accomplish their goals can look drastically different, and BOTH can be successful. It's like those optical illusions where one sees the vase and another sees the profile of two faces. You're both right. Yet so many times in our field, one is favored over the other, and not everyone's perspective or approach are valued.

chapter 4

SELECTION & TRAINING

Recruitment is an important piece of the involvement and leadership development puzzle. It helps us create a pool by which to fill our membership and executive board roles, and allows us to target our work toward those interested in it. However, there may need to be a narrowing of options, and so we select. And once we select, there is a need to bring these new members "on board" the organization- so we train. I am of the belief that selection and training are the area in which introverts are most vulnerable; these processes contain more opportunities for judgment to hinder their progress than any other step we'll explore in this book. In her book The Introvert's Way, Sophia Dembling provides an astute response that could address why these processes often leave our organizations so heavily stocked with extroverts:

> One of the risks of being quiet is that other people can fill your silence with their own interpretations.

You're bored. You're depressed. You're shy. You're judgmental. You have nothing to say. [...] Nature abhors a vacuum, and when other people can't read us, they unite their own story- not always one we would choose or that's true to who we are.

Selection and training provide enough of these silent moments, early enough in a process where we have to speculate on what they might mean, to be problematic. After all, many of the people going through this process might be new, and we don't yet know what to make of their behavior.

She waited a long time to answer that question- she probably didn't prepare.

He's having trouble holding eye contact- he's going to be awkward.

This information's really important, why can't she seem to pay attention?

He hasn't spoken up once; he just doesn't get it, does he?

In the selection process, these quirks reaffirm what we've been taught to see as factors by which to weed down a population; in training, they further cloud our judgment, leaving many to see students as prepared or unprepared, carrying strong potential or needing to be "worked on." As with each section in this book, my goal is to help you examine not just the way you look at students who are participating in these processes, but also the processes themselves.

At the start of each cycle, it's exciting to move from the recruitment stage to selection. It's exhilarating to have options for who will fill our ranks, so we dedicate ourselves to the time-consuming but important work of populating these ranks with the strongest candidates. What steps make up your selection process? They can vary widely depending on the nature of the opportunity, so let's start by addressing some of the most common ones, as well as the challenges that they may present.

The Written Application
Why They Work
In addition to being an efficient way to collect demographic information needed to know who we have in our pool, the written application is designed to get at motivation and provide a glimpse inside the head of the prospective student leader. Again, they provide the fodder to feed the shortcuts we create when seeking to create a cadre of candidates; questions like "What do you hope to get from this position?" and "Why do you want to work with us?" seem to give us the answers we need to focus when it comes time to make decisions in person.

Why Introverts May Struggle
In some ways, introverts don't really struggle in this arena. It's a form of asynchronous communication, which often works to their advantage; answers can be thought out and expressed elegantly, and as such they tend to be strong leaders on paper. The struggle comes later in the selection

process; because they can be time-consuming to review, written applications don't always make it in full to everyone involved in the decision-making process. If an introvert is, in fact, strong on paper, this portion of their record may not be weighed fully by all reviewers, creating a bias toward the portions of the process that they do see.

The Group Interview
Why They Work
Leadership and involvement are, by their very nature, cannot be solitary endeavors. The group interview, and its less structured counterpart the candidate social (see below), is designed to provide interviewers with insight on how students will interact with one another. Students may be asked to make quick decisions, present themselves and ideas, or work together to create something new.

Why Introverts May Struggle
While the group interview does provide valuable information, it can also provide false evidence of how someone will (or won't) interact on a team. Most evaluating performance in this area can identify disengagement as the result of overpowering or domineering individuals; our ability to target a scenario as overwhelming or energy-sapping for introverts is more nuanced, and therefore harder to account for. As such, extroversion inadvertently becomes disproportionately valuable- a valuation that hurts introverts unable to muster the energy required to shine for the length of the activity.

The Individual Interview
Why They Work

The individual interview, when done well, can also be a strength of introverts. With a connection to the interviewers and questions that allow them to bring out their areas of interest and expertise, and the time to appropriately expand on answers, introverts shine in these uninterrupted moments to convey their thoughts.

Why Introverts May Struggle
While verbal cues have the potential to be exemplary, introverts can occasionally be betrayed by how their nonverbal cues are perceived. Taking time to pause and craft an answer can be seen as fumbling, and most of them are aware of that. In those moments, introverts may feel forced to decide which is more acceptable- answering without pausing and being comfortable with whatever may come out, or taking a longer second to compose ideas and risk the perception of stalling.

The Candidate Social
Why They Work
A variation on the group interview, candidate socials are becoming more common as a means to determine how prospective student leaders or members will interact with one another, in the absence of the sort of direction that an interview or team building activity would provide. They are excellent for picking up any pre-existing conflict between students, and can also take off some of the pressure that a competitive selection process might create.

Why Introverts May Struggle
Some may expect that the challenge for introverts in this scenario is to be social with other candidates; for some, that

may be the case, but likely shouldn't be the most common issue to expect. Be careful where in the process, or in a day, you place these socials. Typically, social activities are placed later in the day, to allow for a full business day for students and the professional observers who may also be participating. However, this timing may be difficult for introverts whose energy has already been drained by a busy day. The result could be a listless or already tired introvert, introduced into a situation that further drains their depleted energy reserves. Even if they do like the people they're with, they may not convey that excitement for their exhaustion from outside factors.

The Mock Presentation
Why They Work
Just as with the written application, introverts are likely to thrive in this arena. The ability to speak uninterrupted on a topic of their choosing, or of significant interest, is likely to bring out the best and the most energy in these students- it allows them to engage with ideas, an unequivocal strength.

Why Introverts May Struggle
Presenting these ideas to peers and others judging the quality of their perspective can be daunting for anyone, but is especially daunting for introverts because they are predisposed to dwell on the feedback provided- especially if it's negative. In the absence of a warm environment in which to start a conversation about what they've presented, they may have trouble speaking with the same ease as an extroverted counterpart might.

With the possible challenges set forth, let's now address some of the ways to combat these concerns and ensure a level playing field for all candidates, irrespective of temperament. Some of these are pulled from an interview guide I developed for student and staff interviewers; others are new strategies, shared here for the first time.

Weigh written responses, performance in the group, and individual encounters with equal reverence. I cannot overstate the importance of this first tip. A hallmark of the introverted mind is a heightened performance when given time to think or reflect, a difference that shows up when comparing written responses to in-person performance. However, I've been a part of multiple selection teams that only gave us a resume, in lieu of a full application. I understand that this is designed to save time, and I appreciate the consideration. But if the process in place doesn't allow me to get a full picture of a candidate, I'd much rather take the time needed to make a more informed decision.

To that end, if possible, I'd advise against ruling out students who don't submit a stellar application (unless they haven't followed instructions or clearly indicate that they are unprepared or unqualified). Of course, I would never advocate for a student who was qualified on paper but legitimately couldn't perform in a flexible, spontaneous environment. But I would encourage you to look for understanding of the job responsibilities in person and on paper- and that means letting all members of the selection team see all parts of their presentation, paper goods included.

Temper the atmosphere of the process to create comfort. In baking, to "temper" a substance such as eggs or chocolate is to bring down the temperature gradually to prevent it from breaking or cooking too quickly. Sometimes students, particularly those who are new to the selection process, need us to temper the situation to allow them to be the best versions of themselves. This includes providing guidelines about how information should be submitted and presented in the application process, sharing selection criteria in advance, introducing yourself warmly, welcoming them to the room, and letting them know that the interview is a conversation.

For a group or individual interview, this may mean providing a schedule for the day, as well as how they will be evaluated, in advance- and not just the morning of! For a presentation, be sure to let students know how much time they have, as well as how you will signal them if they are coming close to their time limit. And for applications, make sure that due dates, dropoff points, and any supplemental materials needed are conveyed clearly, multiple times. Ensure students that the process is an open one, and affirm that by being available to answer questions or address concerns.

With that said, this should not be an invitation to not take the process seriously. We need to know that these students are capable of being professional, and an interview is the first place we'll likely get to see that competency from them. Strive to create an environment that is at once professional and as unintimidating as possible. Remember: for some students, this may be the first time they've ever interviewed for anything!

In interview scenarios, patiently allow time for interviewees to respond. Even for the most prepared students, a response to a direct question doesn't always come quickly. Let the candidate know at the outset that it's okay to take a moment to think about a question before responding, and hold true to that promise. Make sure that your nonverbal cues as an observer match this voiced patience- if candidates feel you are getting impatient, it could affect their performance.

Pay attention to how students engage with instructions or information given. Don't take for granted looking away or doodling; both of these quirks are frequently associated with inattention but could actually be signs of the internal processing that yields a stellar response upon reflection. Don't take these cues at face value; see what they produce. It is at that point that you'll be able to tell who is loafing and who is learning.

Even in group interview processes or shared environments, vary planned activities to be both social and solitary. Yes, these scenarios are designed to measure how a candidate will participate in a group. But by allowing for occasional reflection or solitary engagement in that process, you'll be providing a surge of energy for those students whose energy (and good temperament) are challenged by large groups and the expectation of breezy conversation. Even small moments to return to one's own thoughts can provide a boost, and you'll see much more pleasant and engaging exchanges with students as a result.

Provide progress updates at each stage of selection. Especially at the end. As professionals, we can be poor at informing candidates who are no longer in consideration for a role of this fact. Be better than this for students, who deserve the opportunity to learn from this experience. If a student is removed from consideration, be sure to reach out to them to let them know…and offer the opportunity to have a follow-up meeting with them to talk about their candidacy. In addition to this initial notification, offer the opportunity again a few weeks following- they may not be ready or feel informed enough to address the issue right away, but could be more prepared to do so eloquently and less emotionally in time.

Once you have your team selected, the next step will be to formally "onboard" and train this group of students. This step is essential to the team's success- not just for these students, who will depend on you and their experienced peers to integrate them into the existing system, but also for the veteran students who will be bringing these new members into the fold. Even for the most independent leaders who run this training on their own, they may need some guidance on how to structure and present a training schedule. This is a moment where you hold a great deal of power, and we hope you'll use it to advocate for the sanity and energy of all your students- introverts included.

Most training efforts suffer from one or more of the following ailments: too long, too dense, too boring. I'll go through each, as well as the effect it could have on introverts (and, in some cases, all students).

Too Long

In an effort to be considerate of time in the long-term, we try to smash a semester or a year's worth of instructive content into one day, or a multi-day stretch packed into one part of the year. What results is a day or multiple days jam-packed with content, but little time to digest and incorporate it into context where it will be used. This can be difficult for introverts, who need downtime between sessions, and substantial downtime following these long days, A change in timing benefits all students- this extended time could actually drain extroverts as well, who will likely use breaks to work through content with their peers.

Some signs your training is too long: energy will flag for all students, across temperamental lines. Eyes may glaze over, you may see students struggling to stay awake. More subtle signs may include an inability to recall what happened in which session, or even what sessions were offered, when evaluations or reviews are requested.

Too Dense

Closely related to "too long," and often occurring for the same reason, a highly dense training seeks efficiency but can result in glazed-over eyes and yawning mouths. This could be because too much information is being presented in a given amount of time, or it could be because the content is arranged in a confusing or complicated fashion.

Particularly in a time where heightened responsibility is being placed on students in high-risk and high-stakes situations, a training that is too dense can hamper their ability to learn the urgently needed skills and procedures to effectively respond.

Some signs your training is too dense: are lots of questions coming up, even for information you feel you covered adequately? Has this information been covered elsewhere in a longer period of time? When you refer back to this information, do students express surprise that it was addressed previously?

Too Boring

In many ways, the tag of 'boring' can be a combination of the other two factors. The 'b' word often comes into play when students have a difficult time contextualizing the content presented, or don't have an opportunity to see where it will be used. While I don't, and never have, advocated for equating this form of education with entertainment, there is something to be said for presenting information in such a way that students can be motivated to learn it. This may mean challenging the mold in which we frame so many of our onboarding activities.

Some signs your training is too boring: we all know what it looks like, and what the symptoms are.

With the potential problems set forth, let's look to some solutions that could help cure what ails your training program.

IMPORTANT: "telling ain't training." I love this adage, a common one in the professional training world I learned from my friend Laura McClernon, a corporate trainer for Garmin. In her book *Stop Repeating, Start Recording* (a great resource for incorporating e-learning into your programmatic efforts) she urges readers to invoke Stephen Covey's famous adage "begin with the end in mind," and pushes the reader to ask "What do I want trainees to know by the end of this session?" I would take it one step further, and ask what you want your students to be able to do by the end of the session? At some point, training notions were conflated with explaining, lecturing, and in extreme cases pontificating. If you do not have some semblance of an active component in your training- a hands-on component, an activity, a simulation- I would strongly urge you to start over with a goal of adding at least one of these elements to the agenda.

By the way, this isn't the same as soliciting contributions or the time-honored "think, pair, share." Participation and training are two different things. The former transforms attendees into participants, while the latter transforms observers into doers. Information, skills, and abilities shared during a training should be actionable by the time trainees leave. Reframing training with these considerations in mind will make a world of difference when seeking to beat away the boring.

Why This Works for Introverts
For students who are accustomed to engaging with ideas on their own, the prospect of having to do so in a space that's already taxing their energy reserves could diminish

them and their attention span. Further, it respects the time of those who have already read or sought out the information that standard lecture-style training may present. Comparatively, getting to see those ideas play out in action, particularly when the individual gets to be a part of that, can be a confidence building process, and contribute to the practice that makes certain projects commonplace, and therefore less stimulating and easier to complete.

Build in breaks. It may seem counterintuitive to add time to a training to make it less long, and from a temporal standpoint it may be. However, we've all participated in activities and events where time passes effortlessly even when we do so for an extended period of time. These times don't feel long, and this is the sort of feeling we should seek to elicit.

One way to do this is to create time for information, techniques, and ideas introduced to sink in. Allow students to, as they see fit, either work through these ideas with their peers, or reflect independently on how to incorporate this new content into existing routines. When you build in these breaks (15 minutes is a good break, I've been to some events where these breaks are 30 minutes), be sure to explain what attendees can do during this time. I've had students balk at extended breaks, insisting that they don't need that long to go to the bathroom or get coffee. But when the downtime is reframed as reflective or collaborative, they tend to be better received across temperamental lines.

Why This Works for Introverts

When I illustrate this topic to students and staff, I draw an extended comparison between the energy reserves of introverts, and that of a cell phone battery. In the absence of a charger, when your phone battery is in the red, there is little that can be done to will more power into its cells. And once it's gone, it's gone- no matter how much you'd like to answer one more text or attempt one more level of Candy Crush.

Now think about how you feel when you find an outlet and can give your phone even a few minutes on the charger. It doesn't always make a huge difference, but you feel better being able to do it, and that good feeling gives you a little more confidence that you can continue about your day. Think of these 15-30 minute breaks as those short trips to the charger. They provide introverts with a short period of time to collect their thoughts, start assimilating information and procedural knowledge into their reserves, and come to your next session refreshed and...well, recharged.

Build capacity for student-led sessions. Let's face it, professional staff and advisors can lose the room sometimes. However, for students who have been through the processes enough to garner a following with their peers, taking to the front of the room may be a more engaging move to make. Allow your senior-level student leaders to present information; it allows younger leaders to learn from those who use the processes often, and honors the experience that these more seasoned leaders have gained.

A word of warning: building engaging presentations doesn't come naturally, to students or to anyone. We've all sat through enough tedious PowerPoint presentations from colleagues and classmates alike to know. If you plan to put students in front of a room, commit to coaching them on how to create engaging sessions that encourage participation and active learning (not attendance and passive hearing).

Why This Works for Introverts
First and foremost, being able to provide this opportunity for introverts can demonstrate that they can be effective in leadership roles. Even though a 2006 survey of 1500+ senior leaders revealed that nearly 2/3 viewed introversion as an outright barrier to leadership, and a 2002 study by Judge, Bono, and Iles revealed that "extroverted leaders are significantly more likely to (1) emerge as leaders in selection and promotion decisions and (2) be perceived as effective by both supervisors and subordinates", when given the right opportunity introverts can thrive in these roles. The coaching mentioned above will be important for these students; not because they don't possess the skills to take on the challenge, but to engender confidence in their ability to do it and be taken seriously by their peers.

Additionally, their extroverted and ambiverted counterparts need to see introverts in positions of leadership and authority, to believe that this sort of individual can do it. Working with student leaders for so many years has shown me that they create their own definitions of what a leader is, and often they don't include introverted traits in it. By placing your trust and authority in these students, all students can learn their definitions of leadership may be a little short-sighted, and could even include them in a way they didn't previously see possible.

Consider "flipping" training. The traditional model for training, and indeed most teaching, is to do the lion's share of the educating in the classroom, with time outside the classroom spent supplementing that content with practice, application, and other methods of cementing that knowledge. Jon Bergman and Aaron Sams had this to say about the method in Edutopia in 2014:

> Flipped learning is more than just an efficient way to [teach]. It is also an opportunity to take students to deeper levels of comprehension and engagement. One of the most important benefits of flipped learning is that it takes the [teacher] away from the front of the room. No longer is class focused on information dissemination, but instead, time can be spent helping students with difficult concepts and extending the learning to deeper levels.
> Perhaps the greatest benefit of flipped learning is that it gives [teachers] more time to interact with students one-to-one and in small groups. [Teachers] are using the time that was once used for direct instruction in a variety of ways to deepen student learning.

Why This Works for Introverts

I am a proponent of incorporating flipped training methods into these sessions, because I can head off common questions that come up in practice, by letting students arrive at those questions in a forum where they can be answered as they happen, rather than trying to address the question en masse each time it comes up individually. Introverts can thrive in this sort of environment, for a few reasons. First, they will thrive leading these sorts of sessions, as Guy Chmieleski alluded to in 2012:

> While these introverted students may not have the same kind of charisma and/or 'come follow me' kind of aura that some of their extroverted peers might; many will possess a kind of strength, depth, and willingness to take on responsibility (and follow through with the commitment) that will make them incredible leaders [...].

And indeed, it is under the circumstances that flipped learning takes place, where Grant, Gino, and Hoffman found that introverts can thrive in leadership roles. Their research, predicated on dominance complimentarity theory suggests that the more extroverted a leader is, the less [employees] will perceive him or her as receptive to their proactive ideas and suggestions. Comparatively, they found that "less extroverted leaders may be receptive to [employee] proactivity as a valuable source of input, communicating in ways that signal openness and interest."

What does that mean?

It means that when needed to take charge of a learning experience that puts the onus on the learner, and when asked to engage with the ideas that make such an experience work, introverts are naturally born custodians. Additionally, those introverts that balk at the public speaking that is sometimes required for training sessions may feel better prepared for the smaller, one-on-one or one-on-few conversations that this training style tends to foster.

A second reason that introverts may thrive in this environment, both facilitators and participants aside, is because they get to implement the ideas that they're getting from their books, videos, and other materials provided prior to the session. Known primarily for their willingness and propensity to engage with ideas, the ability to put them into action and understand how they'll work in practice will hold their attention better than much of the pontificating that we use as a means to train students.

Not sure where to start with incorporating flipped learning into your upcoming training models? Start by seeking to address these questions:

• What are the learning outcomes of this program? What do I want students to be able to do? Are there concrete skills or procedural knowledge (versus theoretical knowledge) that I expect them to leave with?

• What resources can I bring into the training that will help them do or complete the process I want them to learn?

• What resources can I have them consume, review, or be familiar with before they come to training?

• How can I convey the need to come into the session with this knowledge ahead of time?

- How can I structure the session to allow this review/consumption in the room, if there isn't anything that can be done in advance? (Randy Brown, an elementary school teacher in Washington, executes the "in-flip" in his third grade classroom, where half the class spends time going over the information needed to participate in an activity, while the other half then comes over to put it into action. You could do something like this as an alternative to having students come with information or knowledge, if needed)

- What will students do with the information and the training once they're done? How will I know if those learning outcomes have been met?

INsights: 5 Ways to Select & Train Introverts in Leadership and Involvement Opportunities

1. **Weigh all elements of the application process equally.** Don't discount written applications as a "weed out" tool, or assume them too long to be seen by the entire committee. There may be gold between those pages, don't throw it away!
2. **Provide resources on how to prepare for selection.** Be it a rubric demonstrating what will be examined, or practice interview sessions, introverts and extroverts alike may want the extra practice ahead of the main event.
3. **As the selection process moves forward, keep students abreast of where they stand.** Particularly when elimination does happen, it can be helpful for to

make the process a developmental one. Offer to meet with students to talk about expectations and how they can work to meet them in the future.

4. **Provide ample processing time as training proceeds.** Important information is difficult to absorb and integrate when the brain feels cluttered, overwhelmed, or tired. Combat this natural breakdown by allowing for periodic "jumps" with time away from the group and other stimulators.

5. **Play on strengths of the group.** If you have students who are knowledgeable in a topic, allow them to present. Introverts may benefit from hearing from peers, and may also be able to build confidence and competence by preparing to teach.

chapter 5

ADVISING & SUPERVISION

If there is a "land speed" record for the length of a one-on-one meeting, I probably set it between 2004 and 2006. It was during those years that I spent, on average, nine minutes every two weeks with our graduate advisor Megan, sharing my experiences with her on the board. It wasn't that I didn't have a good experience- I really did. And it wasn't that I didn't have anything to say- sometimes I did. It just wasn't the place for me to say all that I needed to say.

Comparatively, my journal entries (due each month to supplement our one-on-ones and provide guidance for our successors) were rich with detail and provided a much clearer look inside my head and my time in my roles. Yes, this could have to do with my natural writer tendencies, but I happen to believe that this is bigger than that.

I know that having students who clam up in check-in meetings or weekly gatherings can be difficult. I struggle with it at times, even with a clear understanding of what may be causing it. This can be a significant challenge of working with introverts- gathering the information needed to effectively advise or supervise them, from them. But beware- this is also a tendency that contributes to the levied accusation of shyness for many introverts. Over the years, those terms have been wrongfully conflated, leading many to believe that shyness and introversion are one in the same. Setting the record straight here: they are not! In a recent Q&A for her Quiet Revolution website, Susan Cain sets forth the following distinction:

> Introversion is about how we respond to stimulation. introverts feel at their most alive and energetic when we are in quieter environments, because our nervous systems react more to stimulation. And extroverts really crave more stimulation, because their nervous systems need it to stay at their most alive and happy [...] Shyness is different. Shyness is about the fear of negative social judgment. So a shy person will feel uncomfortable in a situation like a job interview or a first date. In practice, there's often an overlap, but not necessarily.

To put it another way, and indeed as Susan has elsewhere- shyness is inherently painful, introversion is not. So your challenge as the advisor or supervisor of an introverted student leader is to create an environment that allows students to be successful and effective in their roles without pushing them to expend an untenable amount of energy in the process.

For all students participating in the important work of getting and staying involved, and developing leadership competencies, a solid relationship with an advisor or supervisor can be a foundation of immeasurable importance. Dunkel and Schuh elaborate on the crucial nature of this relationship in *Advising Student Groups and Organizations*:

> Pascarella and Terenzini (1991) conclude that learning and personal developemnt are enhanced when students are involved in educationally purposeful extracurricular activities. Kuh and Lord (1994) observe that involvement [...] was the single most potent experience associated with the development of practical competence. Practical competence in this case is defined as skills that employers are seeking, in such areas as decision making, leadership, cooperation, and communications. Kuh and Lund also report that participation [in student government] contributes to the development of self-confidence and self-esteem.

They go on to note, "[s]tudents also benefit when they learn skills while working with the organization that can be transferred to their career." And, most importantly, they emphasize the need to adapt style for a diversity of students:

> [n]aturally you will be most comfortable in the role with which you are most familiar; however, you must understand that although comfort in a specific role may diminish your sense of needing to know about other roles, student groups and organizations will

continually challenge you to assume and work with various roles depending on you or your situation.

So for the sake of future prosperity, it is essential that we learn to take note of how to best advise all students we work with. Some areas to take particular note of with introverted students include the nature and structure of their physical work environment, the scope of positional responsibilities, perceptions and definition of participation in activities, assisting them in learning to motivate and lead others, and providing ample opportunities to make meaning of their experiences.

Structure of the Work Environment

How do you encourage your student leaders to work? Moreover, is that seen as the only way they can work? This pair of questions is important to pose early, for the sake of both introverted and extroverted members of student groups and teams; your answers will affect the quality of their work, and the group dynamic in which they produce and complete it.

As individualistic cultures go, we are fairly bullish about encouraging those individuals to work in groups. We're championing open office spaces, we push people to produce viable and effective products and initiatives in groups, and we value highly (perhaps too highly, in my estimation) one's ability to thrive in a group environment. However, I'd also say that we occasionally miscalculate what it takes to work well in that group environment. In the absence of a thoughtfully inclusive selection and training process (see the previous chapter), we end up with a crush of student leaders praised for their desire and ability to effortlessly speak up in a group session, volunteer ideas, and create affable relationships with the people around them. This is great for creating social connections, but isn't always effective when working toward a common goal. Successful work groups need a balance of people who will volunteer ideas and people who will ponder those ideas carefully, people who will speak up and people who will listen, people who will monitor the social temperature of a group and people who will keep their progress and output on track.

As I've said, the latter part of each of those sentences is not outside of the abilities of any extrovert, nor is the ability to serve in the former role out of bounds for an introvert. There is value in pushing people to develop competencies that stretch their natural preferences, as all people will need all of those skills. But again, the key word here (and always) is ease. It is easy for introverts to serve in those latter roles; their sensibilities are built for it and it provides them more energy than serving in the alternate position. Why wouldn't you want someone to serve in a role that they'd do well in easily?

As an advisor who must balance the needs of creating accessible and communal spaces, while also serving as a co-custodian of student energy and temperamental needs, what can you do?

Set and uphold standards for communal space. Just as residence halls have designated quiet hours that (presumably) are enforced by professionals in that space, consider setting similar boundaries and norms for communal workspaces that student leaders inhabit. Corporate coworking spaces are proliferating rapidly in major cities in large part because of their ability to balance the needs of communal and solitary professionals. Some spaces are marked as open, where talking, conversation, and even debate can take place; however, there are also spaces designated as "quiet," and rooms can be reserved for temporary "noise" such as conference calls, personal phone calls, and meetings. Allow and encourage headphone use for those who seek to block out external noise, and designate certain time blocks each day for "quiet work." Uphold the expectation that louder or more potentially disruptive activities take place elsewhere. These norms, and their reliable enforcement, will help create an understanding that you recognize the diversity of needs for productivity, and students will appreciate it (even if they don't do so vocally or demonstrably!).

Identify and advertise workspace alternatives. Ensure that alternate spaces to complete work, such as library carrels, reservable study spaces, or even scheduled spaces like conference or meeting rooms, are known as additional options in which to do work. This way, if a student needs time and space to take what Cain calls 'deep dives' into information or a given project, a plan can be established, rather than a hasty retreat in a moment of overwhelm, which often tends to have social implications (such as assumptions of anger, frustration, or isolation). Help manage these assumptions by endorsing the use of these spaces, and advocating strongly for their use to all students that could benefit from solitude in their daily routine.

Educate students about differences in individual work style. Helping students to understand one another can go a long way in helping create space where all can work effectively. This can be done during training, or in other supplementary training opportunities that your office, department, or organization may provide. Even as students of all temperaments (extrovert, introvert, or ambivert) start to understand themselves, they may still need coaching and reminders of how their style interacts with the others; seek to head off stylistic clashes by helping them learn what to expect, how they could be perceived, and how they can adjust their style to best collaborate with others.

Surprise! Other Duties as Assigned

As I alluded to in the chapter on recruitment, the makeup and structure of any given student position can provide insight into the goals that the individual should be expected to meet. It is human nature to rely on a defined scope of activity, even if duties or expectations may occasionally stray away from what was originally set. And although there isn't a way to prevent from all additional responsibilities that may arise (nor should there be, as this is a part of life and we should not seek to insulate students from that inevitability), there are ways to manage the disruption that this change in expectations or plans that this could present.

If possible, provide advance notice. Many of us have been told to minimize surprises when striving to be a good employee to our managers; the same can be true for those who we advise or supervise. If a change in policy or procedure is on the horizon, and the change is not explicitly a confidential one, try to warn students that something different is on the horizon. Because introverts thrive in environments with routine (it reduces the stimulation needed to operate in a world that isn't always predictable), changes to this routine can cause their stimulation to spike and their work may suffer as a result. But when notice is given that something will be changing, they can start to adapt to how that new wrinkle or policy may affect their modus operandi.

Work closely with students to help them align skills to new responsibilities. Whenever new responsibilities or elements are added to a process, it's important to check in often and see how students are doing with the change. But it is of particular importance that we check in with introverts - not to ensure that they understand, but to make sure that they still feel effective and empowered in their role. Because introverts are accustomed to most of their dialogue being internal, they don't always speak up right away if they're having trouble. This could be solved by providing additional tutorials in a number of formats- written, video, infographic, etc., but these supplemental tools should be supplemented with conversations in which we assess their comfort and efficacy.

Provide personal connections to help them adjust. As the chapter on Recruitment offers, introverts buck the stereotype of being anti-social when they have cultivated relationships with individuals. Peer mentors have proven especially powerful in the involvement experience, and can continue to be helpful here. Pair more experienced student leaders with younger or newer ones in an informal mentorship program, or, should you have a more formal one, assign those leaders to office hours or "office calls" to check in on student leaders when policy changes are announced. Empower them to troubleshoot their peers' concerns, answer questions, and to inform you of the pulse of the affected population. Here again, this personal touch can lower the threat of feeling alone in struggling,

Meeting Participation

A 2015 sketch by the comedy duo *Key and Peele* received a special commendation of sorts in the introvert community for showing (in a highlight format a la the ESPN news program SportsCenter) a teacher calling on an introverted student whose hand was not raised, because she noticed that he was otherwise engaged. "That's Teacher of the Year material, right there!", fictional commentator Boyd Maxwell exclaims, and he's not wrong. A tremendous amount of pressure is placed on appearing participatory in classroom and meeting scenarios, and any behaviors seen outside of what we traditionally view as "engaged" are deemed inattentive at best, and hostile or combative at worst. Just because a student doesn't raise a hand to answer every question, or volunteer ideas with ease, doesn't mean he or she isn't actively on board with the meeting's proceedings. I address this concern often, and feel that much of the counsel provided there for efficacy in staff meetings, can also be applicable for student-run meetings. As you coach student leaders, consider helping them to run meetings that are inclusive of how introverts may behave in these scenarios.

Meeting organizers, if you will be working with an agenda, send it out in advance. My agendas draw liberally from the minutes of the previous meeting, but also include cartoons or funny pictures to show a sense of humor about the work we do. Familiarity with what issues will be discussed and what questions will be asked could help reduce the disorientation that comes with spontaneous lines of questioning; the personal touch provides a reminder that you recognize the humanity of the people you're working with. What's more, meetings can move more quickly if people are able to plan their responses. If you are not an agenda user, even a quick overview of what questions might be raised during the meeting could suffice. Returning for just a moment to the quick operational definition of introversion ("easily overstimulated"), the preparation phase for a meeting can help mitigate that potential shock that comes with an unanticipated query.

Consider a preamble or foreword to the meeting. Any information that may need to be known in advance of discussion (changing climate for a decision, factors to consider when assigning tasks) should be provided at the outset of the meeting. Some may argue that the information could be sent out over email; in some cases that could be appropriate. However, when the background information is sensitive to tone, electronic communication may need to be eschewed in favor of a more expressive medium. Other tips for running "introvert-friendly meetings":

Try to structure the meeting in such a way that the flow of information is logical. Here again, the shift from one item to the next can be difficult to wrap one's head around, for introverts and extroverts alike. Even if disjointed topics can't be arranged thematically, consider a chronological or priority based arrangement of agenda items. If the system can be understood, this can help an introvert be more present during these gatherings.

Give these meetings the time they truly deserve. Too often, meetings discourage dialogue where it may be needed, for the sake of time. But it should be noted that in sacrificing length of conversation, rushed meetings could also cheat introverts out of an opportunity to contribute. To communicate well, time is needed to process information, but also to craft our responses. Make sure the efficient structure of your meeting isn't at the expense of a rich, meaningful and necessary discussion.

End the meeting with a review of action steps. Much like a dissertation or other scholarly publication concludes with implications and next steps, meetings can as well. After a period where information has been fed in a steady stream, the clarity that can come from a quick summary or explicit voicing of action steps is invaluable- I would imagine that even extroverts would appreciate that summation of the meeting's events.

Include these tips in training that you provide students on how to engage their peers; these strategies will serve them well in their present role, as well as meetings they may run as future supervisors.

Helping Introverts Motivate Others

As the chapter on selection and training reveals, we are quick to place extroverts in positions of leadership because they are easier for us to see and hear when it comes time to make these decisions. And indeed, a 2006 study by Jones* notes that in a survey of 1500 senior leaders earning at least six-figure salaries, 65% viewed introversion as a significant hurdle to overcome when developing leadership; only 6% of that same group believed that introverts could be more effective in a leadership capacity than their extroverted counterparts. However, despite pervasive attitudes to the contrary, Grant, Gino, and Hofmann's 2011 research reveals that introverts can thrive in leadership roles, when the right circumstances are provided:

> When employees take charge to introduce new work methods, less extraverted leaders may embrace their ideas, using them to develop more efficient and effective systems (Moon, Kamdar, Mayer, and Takeuchi, 2008), correct errors in faulty procedures (Staw and Boettger, 1990), and identify new techniques for preventing errors and problems in the future (Wall, Jackson, and Davids, 1992). Furthermore, less extraverted leaders may take particular notice of employee efforts to voice important problems, which can enhance group performance (Detert and Burris, 2007; Van Dyne and LePlne, 1998), and respond to upward influence by mobilizing attention and effort toward solving problems, which can enable them to make

meaningful changes with respect to strategically significant issues (Dutton, et. al., 2001).

That is to say, when it comes to creating environments where employees are self-sufficient and empowered to speak up to create meaningful change, introverts can excel in a supervisory role. With that said, introverted students may need help cultivating the skills to (a) recognize this potential in themselves, and (b) to weaponize these skills in real-world leadership scenarios. How can you, as an advisor or supervisor, contribute to the development of this dynamic?

Educate on the nuance of personality style, highlighting the strengths of each type.
No broad group, be it based on race, sexual orientation, gender, or temperament, should be treated as a monolith. And indeed, no two introverts are alike. Even if you use the textbook definition as defined by Myers-Briggs, that still leaves you with eight different types of introversion (due to its interaction with the other dimension of personality type). It's easy to make assumptions that not all introverts want to speak publicly, run meetings, or serve in high-profile leadership positions. Even those who are introverts can occasionally get trapped in the belief that all introversion is the same "variety" as theirs. I urge you to challenge yourself to look beyond that belief, and to encourage others to be similarly open to what introversion could look like. You will have some students who speak little and prefer to write their thoughts down, but you may also have introverts that easily articulate their thoughts but need a considerable "recharging" time to maintain that sort of energy. Both

types, and many others, are legitimate- as always, it's all about where and how you're most energized.

There are elements of the involvement and leadership experience that introverts excel at naturally, and it benefits all members of a group to find places to let those traits shine. The patient listening that introverts are innately excellent at, hold value when making complicated decisions that require consideration for many opinions and sources of information. Their propensity to dive deeply into a topic of interest makes them excellent candidates to educate their peers. And when given space to share their thoughts and feelings without interruption, they can provide valuable insight to a group. But for all of this to happen successfully, groups need to be constructed in such a way that these skills and abilities are valued and permitted to coexist with "traditional" leadership qualities. Advisors and supervisors can take the lead in cultivating the environment accepting of all these traits.

Emphasize the importance of listening as a tool in the leadership utility belt.
Less extraverted individuals tend to spend more time listening and less time talking (Ramsay, 1996), and feel more apprehensive about initiating communication in groups (Opf and Loffredo, 2000) and speaking in public (Feingold, 1983). As a result, less extraverted leaders may send more verbal and nonverbal signs that they are open to proactivity and may take more time to hear and consider ideas and suggestions. A heightened capacity for focus, combined with a desire to take in information, makes introverts well-equipped to hear and operationalize what's presented to

them; in a paradigm of leadership that increasingly values that ability, introverts are poised to be coveted highly in leadership roles.

Incorporate teaching on creativity into your own training.

[...] even when employees' proactive behaviors are not relevant to organizational goals, there are two reasons to believe that less extraverted leaders will respond to them in ways that enhance group performance. First, because less extraverted leaders listen more carefully, employees will be more likely to feel that their ideas are considered and appreciated, which will enhance and sustain their motivations to contribute (e.g. Dutton, et. al., 2001; McFarlin and Sweeney, 1996). Second, even if employees proactive suggestions are misguided, they can still facilitate constructive changes. Employees' proactive behaviors can introduce a novel perspective, which may "stimulate divergent attention and thought. As a result, even when they are wrong they contribute to the detection of novel solutions and decisions that, on balance, are qualitatively better" (Nemeth, 1986: 23).

Creating Reflection Opportunities

Making meaning of an experience or opportunity doesn't come naturally to many students; indeed, many of them have lived lives that allowed them to move quickly through a crush of experiences without taking time to examine how they into their lives. All students will benefit from the contextualization of their time with you, but introverts in particular will thrive when given the chance to examine their progress and take lessons away from it. However, the pacing and workload of many involvement and leadership opportunities delays this crucial element. Normalizing this time-consuming but rewarding piece of the involvement experience can yield better work habits, provide intermediate opportunities for "course correction" prior to more regimented evaluation schedules (see next chapter), and prompt students to make decisions about how aspects of the experience will fit into their college careers, post-collegiate plans, and beyond. But it all starts with the decision to try.

First, voice that these opportunities are necessary.
The implication in this directive, of course, is that you do deem these reflection opportunities necessary. And if you still don't buy into the strategy yet, consider the words of Simon Sinek, author of *Start with Why*: "We are drawn to leaders and organizations that are good at communicating what they believe. Their ability to make us feel like we belong, to make us feel special, safe and not alone is part of what gives them the ability to inspire us." Our students will need to be these people when they graduate from our halls and move on to offices, labs, and careers that will push them to not only make their own meaning, but to seek that meaning in others. Help them understand that they will need to be able to articulate the significance of their experience-in job interviews, applications for funding, papers during post-collegiate study, and other places; and that the ability to do that effectively comes from knowing what you're doing and why.

Additionally, these captured reflections can be invaluable for transition. The transient nature of students can make continuity difficult for student leaders, and their successors in a role may not always get proper training or introduction to their new duties. Sharing excerpts of student reflections can be helpful to show them not just the mechanical "how-to" pieces of their role, but also how their predecessor came to be successful in it, and overcame struggle when needed. It is imperative to normalize struggle when someone is doing something new, and (if they consent, of course!) your road-tested leaders can do that for their peers by engaging in reflection in a public or shareable forum.

Next, create time for them.
The true power of any given directive is tested by how it is upheld, not just how it is unveiled. Just as it seems odd when someone tells us they don't mind that we're running late as they sigh heavily, or can tell something is not okay even as their words say they are, it is disingenuous to espouse the importance of reflection, and then build a schedule that doesn't support its occasionally time-consuming nature. Are there quick moments in meetings where you can allow students to jot down early thoughts or share them in an activity? Can you set an expectation that these reflections happen outside meetings or events and are submitted later? Consider the makeup of your group and the scope of their responsibility as you set these expectations. For some groups it may make sense to leave a few minutes at the end of some meetings to work as a group to reflect; for others, it may make more sense to make the process individual and "outside work."

Most importantly, set a realistic timetable for these reflections to be completed. While it is true that introverts are adept at making meaning of their experiences, it is also true that their abilities to do so are hindered when they don't have the time to truly discern what that meaning is. Set a time that makes sense for your organization and its goals, but also recognize that sometimes 48-72 hours may not be enough to truly encapsulate impact. Seek for a length of time that is cognizant of overall aims, without taking so long that the true impact of the experience is lost by memory.

Allow for multiple forms of reflection.

In *Quiet Influence*, Jennifer Kahnweiler illuminates six strengths of the introverted, two essential ones for this conversation being Focused Conversation and Writing*. In the former, she cites introverts' ability to carry meaningful conversations with one another that avoid the tedious and fear-inspiring "small talk" step. This can be a wonderful conduit for meaningful reflection, through the oft-used "one-on-one meeting" strategy. Those who advise or supervise in a manner that uses the one-on-one meeting already hold a powerful venue for reflection.

For my part, when I think about the one-on-one meetings that I blew through so quickly, I recall the moments that I got to discuss findings and excerpts from my journals as the most impactful ones on my development and understanding. When given the opportunity to speak and write, I was able to think more clearly, reply more eloquently, and remember solutions that I wanted to pose with more ease. If you have students who struggle to fill the moments of your meetings with words, I urge you to consider letting them supplement the spoken word with other forms of expression. I like to think that Kahnweiler's latter strength, that of Writing, is a catch-all term to include any asynchronous forms of communication that students may employ to express their feelings. Writing, yes, is often described as a strength of introverts, but this could also just as easily be expressed through drawing, doodling, or even "delayed" speech like videos or podcasts. The time to think and compose thought, verbally or otherwise, is undoubtedly an asset when seeking the highest quality response from an introvert.

As business is being done, be sure to also make time to learn about students as individuals- as students, friends, and community members- and then pose questions about their work with you that will allow those roles to intertwine. Ask the student working on her thesis how her research is going and where she's seen the research pop up in daily life. Talk to the student employee who you've seen in a Los Pollos Hermanos T-shirt what he thought about the end of *Breaking Bad*. Remember that a student group has a competition coming up, and wish them luck before they leave. This rapport building makes the inevitable face-to-face interactions less clinical and more approachable. By providing opportunities to talk out these connections, two important things will happen: (1) you will capture the oft-ignored introverts who do prefer to talk things out, but for whom that is an energy-sapping process; and (2) you will provide much-needed practice for students to draw connections between prior experiences and future pursuits, an invaluable skill when becoming a good interviewer.

Bring these opportunities into the evaluation and assessment process.

In our next chapter, we will explore how you can best evaluate and assess an introvert's work. A benefit of encouraging reflection in the process of advising, is giving those who need more time to ponder their answers an "approved" means by which to do so. Encouraging periodic reflection during the involvement and leadership process will provide much needed downtime to develop and articulate ideas on how their experiences have affected them. Further, having a recorded form of reflection (journals, blogs, vlogs, social media posts, etc.) can be considered during these evaluations. The burden on students to produce a satisfactory answer in the moment, can be lessened when their progress over the course of the year can be weighed in the evaluation process as well.

INsights: 5 Ways to Advise & Supervise the Leadership and Involvement of Introverts

1. **Create and cultivate a workspace respectful of introverts.** Balance ease of access with peers and authority figures, with respect for stimulating elements like interruptions or excess noise.
2. **If new duties appear on the horizon, help minimize the concerns that they may cause.** Provide additional training, let experienced leaders share their wisdom and lessons, do what it takes to keep additional responsiblilty from crossing the line between challenging and overwhelming.

3. **Craft and conduct introvert-friendly meetings.** Notice and agenda sharing ahead of time, creating a multitude of contribution opportunities during, and following up on assigned duties and ideas after, can help introverts lose less energy during meetings and gatherings.

4. **Help introverts use their "powers" to inspire and encourage others.** Introverts who have parlayed their personality and aspirations into involvement and leadership success can serve as an invaluable resource to those students contemplating taking on such a role. Providing structured moments when this mentoring and counseling can take place between students creates mutually beneficial relationships.

5. **Intentionally make space for these leadership and involvement experiences to be reflected upon.** In the absence of time to look back on leadership and involvement, introverts may have difficulty making meaning of, and finding significance in, what may be outstanding work. Underscore the importance of this critical step in the involvement experience by being vocal about its necessity and reserving time for it in the course of performing a role.

GUEST CHAPTER: THE INTROVERT CREATIVE CONNECTION
by Sue Caulfield

While there isn't a direct correlation between introversion and creativity, clear benefits have been shown in encouraging students of all temperaments to access their creative side. Here, Sue Caulfield brings you her take on the Introvert Creative Connection and how it affects student involvement and leadership.

When Amma's posed the question in *The I's Have It* of how introversion is affected by the other aspects of personality type, I had a very visceral reaction:

> [when asked what happens when stimulation becomes too much] I am unable to focus on anything, make tons of mistakes, miss details, and can't get in touch with my F.

While it may seem silly to refer to different parts of a singular being by "my I" or "my F", these different parts of a type have a delicate interplay in many introverts.

I was instantly transported to my senior year of college. It was a Wednesday afternoon and our Student Council meeting was just wrapping up. From a Student Council President point of view, this meant that my next few hours looked something like this; check in with my Executive Board and get their feedback from the meeting, hang around and answer any questions that Class

Representatives have, check in with our new Freshmen Representative to make sure they weren't overwhelmed, talk to the Programming Chair about this weekend's event, talk to the Community Service Chair about next weekend's events, grab some sort of cheap sustenance (read: junk food) and run over to my evening 3-D Art and Sculpture Class.

While my studio classes were always this sacred space in my undergraduate career, I can't help but look back on those particular Wednesday evening classes and note that I struggled the most in this particular one. I was uninspired, drained and cranky. Creating sculpture interesting me, but I wanted to take a nap in whatever materials I had instead. When I became incredibly emotional one evening over a clay pot, my professor realized that something was up. After a ramble that involved the upcoming Halloween party, Student Council open positions, some sniffles and my inability to hot glue piece of glass to a teddy bear, his eye softened. "Sue, you are f*cking exhausted. Go home now, get a good night's sleep and try to work a nap into your schedule every Wednesday. The teddy bear can wait until next week."

(I don't think I ever thanked this teacher properly, so if you are reading this, I am sorry for getting snot on your dress shirt.)

A drained battery is a very real and dangerous thing for many introverts. The next Wednesday, I took a nap in my car in the Molloy College parking lot prior to my Wednesday night class. Over the next few weeks, that twenty minute rest time became the most protected time on my calendar. My friends and colleagues in the Student Services Department joked that I was similar to a famous president who needed his afternoon naps. It wasn't long before I saw a difference in my temperament during my night class... and I wasn't the only one who noticed. My professor smiled one evening during the end of the semester as I excitedly explained an idea for my thesis in the spring. I thought his pleasant nature was solely due to my chipper conversation until I realized I had bedhead from my beloved car nap.

Looking back on that evening class, I am not sure I really realized that it was my introverted nature that was being effected by my hectic schedule. However, when it took a toll on my ability to be creative, I knew that something needed to change. In speaking with other introverts who also have creative tendencies, I have realized that the two are intertwined in an intimate manner. This delicate balance between nurturing one's introverted needs and allowing one's creative capacity to flourish is a topic that I am familiar with both personally and professionally. It is a phenomenon that I lovingly refer to as the Introverted Creative Connection (ICC). It is my hope that by discussing details of the Introverted Creative Connection that we can be more aware of it for the populations that we serve as higher education professionals. Even more so, I hope this chapter will help shed some light on those senior art students who need that staff member to pull them aside and tell them to take a nap so their inner artist can heal and continue to Light It Up.

Opting In...trovertedly

Conversation about any given individual's creative bandwidth has been around for decades. Investigation into creative nature, what can make someone 'more creative' than someone else and exposure to different creative stimuli are all topics that have been discussed at great length. However, there seems to be one aspect to creativity that has gotten mixed reviews: introversion. The intersect between introversion and creativity seems to be somewhat of a mystery for many individuals.

For starters, I would like to point out that this intersection exists for everyone BUT it may look different for everyone. Similar to how there is a scale for introversion and extroversion, I think that there is also a scale for creativity that aligns with these two preferences.

Because I think in pictures, here's a visual example:

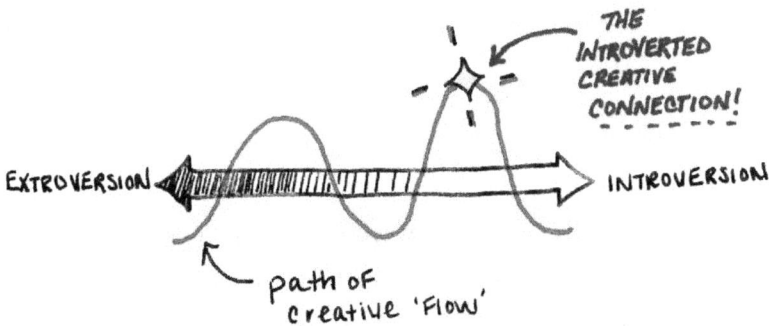

THE INTROVERTED CREATIVE CONNECTION!

EXTROVERSION ◄————————————————► INTROVERSION

path of creative 'Flow'

Because this is a book chapter, here's a written example:
During a Creative Writing class, a profession assigns the first small group project of the semester. The professor creates

the groups and the assignment - a short screenplay. She's elated to find out that she's paired with four other class partners and can't wait to get together to discuss ideas. After their small group meeting, everyone in the group decides to take a section of their assignment, write a first draft and then critique the pieces. Inspired by the conversation and interplay between the individuals, she suggests that they write a script now and rehearsal it amongst themselves. The group agrees and spins off one another's suggestions for the remainder of the afternoon.

One could argue that this student prefers to process outwardly and the influence of the group causes a spark in her creative process. By continuing to feed off the group influence, this student feels energized and inspired.

Another might argue that the group was small enough for this student to cause inspiration as opposed to exhaustion. By taking the time to write on their own and then receive feedback, it provided the right amount of privacy for this student to produce quality work. The intimate nature of the feedback was comfortable enough for this student to continue to produce.

I'm here to tell you that both of those are probably correct, and that it truly doesn't matter which scenario is correct. What matters is that this student has options. And options are the very reason why creativity can thrive. These options are vital to a student's time in AND out of the classroom. If we want our students to thrive as creative individuals and impactful leaders, then we need to give them options to do so.

Types and Strengths

In September 2014, Amma wrote a blog post "Cross Training For Creativity," inspired by Megan, a friend who is an avid runner. Megan spoke about how cross-training is vital for a runner's desired physical outcome in many race scenarios. Amma took this cross-training reference and applied it to creativity, comparing the effects to working in higher education. Amma successfully pointed out that by taking part in hobbies and interests outside of your dedicated career, an individual can flex one's creative muscle.

This image of flexing creative muscles is used quite often when discussing creativity. From personal experience, I can certainly say that creative acts do not just 'happen.' Often, it takes multiple tiny acts to build these creative muscles and even more training to sustain them for the long term. This 'flexing' that we witness in the product of creative acts is not very far off from what happens in our heads during this training period.

When an individual intentionally practices creative acts, the brain is challenged. It is asked to make new connections, find different solutions and think in ways that it normally may not think. It lights up and new pathways are formed.

Now, I'm not going to get into the different chemical interactions involved in this intricate process. However, if you are interested in how introverts and extroverts are uniquely different in how they chemically process stimuli, I highly recommend reading Marti Olsen Laney's The *Introvert Advantage*. Laney goes into the nitty gritty of how introverts and extroverts have different preferred neurological pathways, and the explanation Amma gives when she distinguishes the two is heavily influenced by Laney's research.

What most resonated with me from Laney's explanations was how introverts are wired with an energy conserving system (introverts run off of the chemical acetylcholine and have a high sensitivity to dopamine). One of my favorite sayings when making a decisions is that "I need to let this marinate." (I'm half Italian, hence the cooking reference. Plus, marinate...yum.) Quite literally, as an introvert, I actually need to let thoughts swirl around until my brain comes up with a solution that is satisfactory. Introverts have this ability through hardwiring to turn inward. This relationship with the inward self is the perfect environment for creativity to flourish.

In the same way that creativity benefits from having options, it also thrives from situations where it derives some extra strength. For example, introverted individuals may experience an extra boost of creativity after some designated quiet time. They may find that without this time, they are unable or struggle to come up with new ideas or make connections to develop solutions.

There is one characteristic where creativity and introversion have unyielding common ground. In both areas, the theme of *complexity* is mentioned time and time again. Mihaly Csikszentmihalyi writes about creative individuals are having a complexity that translates to multitudes. In other words, instead of having the characteristics of one individual, creatives seem to embody more than that. This complexity often transfers to their work, resulting in unique content and products.

In the same vein, introverts are often described as having a certain complexity to their personalities. I believe that this complexity stems from the fact that the majority of introverts have highly sensitive personalities (HSPs). Amma writes about this phenomenon far less often, but a great primer on the concept can be found in Elaine Aron's 1996 *The Highly Sensitive Person*, as well as Aron's continued writings on it*. While high sensitivity makes sense to individuals who have this trait, it can be difficult to understand for individuals without this characteristic. This sensitivity, paired with the inward nature of an introvert can attribute to the complexity that Csikszentmihalyi identifies.

In additional to this complexity, it has been noted that both creatives and introverts value time spent alone. For introverts, this is coveted recharging time. For creatives, it qualifies as the same and sometimes more. This is where the writing, painting and music making can happen (to use some concrete examples of creative acts). This alone time is also imperative to creatives honing a new skill. We will talk more about this later in the chapter.

As you can see, there are several strengths that are common in both introverts and creatives. By harnessing these strengths, introverted creatives can derive

Harnessing the ICC

Now that the overlap between introversion and creativity has been defined, I'd like to talk about two specific tools that individuals can used to harness the Introvert Creative Connection. It is imperative to foster environments that play off of these strengths and using these tools can help individuals do just that.

Woodshedding

The first situational tool is one that I did not have a name for until listening to one of my favorite podcasts, Invisible Office Hours. (Sidenote: Highly recommend this podcast for creative entrepreneurs - go listen!) The fifth episode from season one is called Internet Woodshedding. In it, Paul Jarvis and Jason Zook talk about the skill of woodshedding, which stems from the music industry. Woodshedding is when a creative takes time to go somewhere private and either learn a new skill and then hone that skill before releasing it into the world. Paul and Jason go on to talk about different projects that they have worked on and how woodshedding has benefiting them in their careers.

Woodshedding is a tool that I have used personally. When I first learned to paint, I spent hours with canvases spread all over my apartment floor. I would paint one, stare at it and move onto the next. These pieces were not shared with anyone until I found one that was somewhere suitable. Even then, I only shared it with a close companion and my studio professor for feedback. After that, I repeated the process until I was ready to share this skill with the world.

Feeding off that natural ability to turn inward, woodshedding can be a powerful tool for introverted creatives. First, it allows these individuals to spend time in a quiet space. Furthermore, introverted creatives can often feel guilt associated with spending time alone instead of with other creatives. This is a 'free pass,' of sorts because their time alone is spent working on their craft. This time working also allows these individuals to practice or build multiple drafts of a project before releasing it to the world. Being that introverts can take criticism personally, this time to perfect their product puts them in a better state of mind. Not only are introverted creatives refreshed, but more confident in their abilities by the time the woodshedding period is over.

Partnerships

In Joshua Wolf Shenk's *Powers of Two; Finding the Essence of Innovation In Creative Pairs*, he writes extensively about famous creative partnerships. Lennon and McCartney, Brennan and Chappelle, Lewis and Tolkien, Marie and Pierre Curie - the list goes on and on. In each of these creative pairs, Shenk discusses how these pairs fulfill different archetypes and how there is a delicate interplay between the creative forces involved. He shows how each pair goes through six stages of creative intimacy as their relationships grow. What is clear between all of these pairs is the tangible about of trust between the pairs. This intimate level of trust manifests in various ways that vary between each pair.

What is most fascinating about Shenk's discoveries is his definition of creative pairs. At one point in the book, Shenk goes on to explain that this pair does not have to be another individual - it can be the relationship that one has with oneself. While he does spend most of his time talking about two separate individuals, this is a crucial point for introverted creatives. One's relationship with oneself is of the utmost importance in general. In addition, it is clear that for introverted creatives, this relationship must be nurtured and cared for as if it were an intimate relationship with another being. Taking the time to care of oneself can have an immediate impact on one's creative skills.

As far as the relationship between creative pairs, I have been very fortunate to personally experience a few fulfilling creative partnerships. (Amma, you're not allowed to edit this out.) One of my most successful partnerships has been with the author of this book, Amma Marfo. Each of us has written about this on our blogs after one of our first projects*. As Shenk points out in Powers of Two, our relationship is one of deep trust. In additional to leaning on each other which various projects, I know that Amma will always take my ideas and let them marinate. She delivers thoughtful feedback and will challenge my ideas while being sensitive to my introverted creative self. Our creative interplay has been one that has strengthened over a period of time that has been comfortable for both of us.

Finding these partnerships for introverted creatives can be essential to an individual's growth. Partnerships allow intimacy and can be comforting for introverted creatives. Having these partners to fall back on in times of need Is incredibly helpful for introverted creatives.

Introverted Creative Students

The Introverted Creative Connection can exist in any individual in any field. It is not limited to individuals in traditional creative environments or industries. Harnessing the power of the Introverted Creative Connection in higher education can set up our introverted creative students for success throughout their education time with us and beyond.

Knowing that these introverted creative students exists within our populations, it is the job of the higher education professional to foster environments where these students thrives. We can use what we know about the Introverted Creative Connection to help create these environments for our students. In addition to quiet spaces, smaller groups and events tailored for intimacy, we can incorporate opportunities for creativity.

A Partnered Approach

One of the first steps to include introverted creative students is to take advantage of the need for creative partnerships. This can be managed in a multitude of ways. Whether it be a professional at the institution, a mentor or a relationship with an upperclassmen, introverted creative students can benefit from a close partnership. Students should be encouraged to actively seek these partners and we can help provide venues to do so.

In student affairs, a natural pathway exists to help introverted creative students find these partnerships. Our classrooms are flexible and so are our curriculums. By infusing the option to accommodate introverted creative needs into our events, we can naturally attract students looking for these partnerships. As professionals, looking for these natural spaces - a comfortable corner during the annual club fair, a poetry reading with a limited number of tickets, televising an event featuring a two on two match - and advertising them to students who can benefit can go a long way.

These partnerships can also help introverted creative students find leadership opportunities and thrive in them. I distinctly remember running through the entire student council agenda with a close friend of mine when I served as SGA president. Not only did this allow me to have a rough draft of what the meeting would look like, but it also gave me the opportunity to anticipate the reactions of my peers. I also got to share some of my out-of-the-box ideas with her prior to the meeting. Having this one on one opportunity relaxed me prior to my speaking engagement. I drew energy from this interaction and used it during meetings.

Introverted creative students can also benefit from these partnerships in another scenario - stuckness. As far as I know, every college student ever has gotten stuck during their academic career in one point or another. Whether its graduate or undergraduate, academic or otherwise, socially or interpersonally, stuckness happens. For introverted creative students, the state of stuckness may be slightly complicated or induced by their creative tendencies. This can compound the state of stuckness and manifest in several ways during college. Having a partner to turn to in times of stuckness can really help a student during this battle. Not only does it give them someone to confide in during times of need, but the intimate nature of this relationship and that trust can give them something to lean on.

Leading Creatively

Leadership for an introverted creative student may push the boundaries of what traditional student leadership looks like. For example, introverted creatives may prefer to work with smaller teams for longer periods of time. Instead of brainstorming as a group, they may find it beneficial to brainstorm alone or with one partner. Then, they could call the group back together, discuss the ideas and take some more time to reflect on each idea. This process could go through several iterations until the project that they are working on is ready to be revealed.

Introverted creative leaders might work better with nontraditional tools at their disposal. Visual tools are a great example of something that could enhance the group's experience. They may ask a group member to take notes in the form of graphic recording. Perhaps they could have each group member record a short video about their idea and play it for the group. Perhaps they prefer to create a jingle or advertisement about their idea which can later be used as advertisement.

An introverted creative student may be better suited in a leadership role for a long term project. Working with a close team could allow for relationship intimacy that is craved. A new project or project that is being rebranded could be the perfect opportunity for this type of student. Keeping all of this in mind can help professionals identify which leadership roles introverted creatives can thrive in.

Recognizing the ICC in Your Space

Identifying a student's type does not mean that this student (or any individual) is limited to that type. As Joshua Wolf Shenk points out in Powers of Two, creatives need on going interactions between the inter- and intrapersonal. This translates to introverted creatives needing both external and internal influences, even though they may prefer one over the other. Introverted preferences should be used to empower creativity, not the opposite.

The Introverted Creative Connection is something that has personally defined who I am as an individual, a professional and an artist. The connection between these two personality preferences is a powerful one and one that can be nurtured. I hope that by revealing a little bit about the ICC in this chapter that you will continue to discover new ways that it benefits you and your students.

chapter 6

EVALUATION & ASSESSMENT

"Time to wake up, campers!
Today is evaluation day. The key word here is 'value.' Do you
have any?"

Modern philosopher and evil weight-loss camp owner Tony
Perkis started the day this way for his young charges in
1993's Heavyweights. While several of his methods proved
to be ill-advised, the gravity he placed on evaluation is all
too real. We may not be assessing the performance of our
student leaders by making them get on a scale publicly, but
the process can create similar vulnerability for students, can
make them feel equally exposed. For many of the leaders
we work with, this formal process of evaluation can be the
first time they learn the impact their performance has had.
How will you choose to initiate and sustain these
conversations?

As with several of the other elements of the student leadership experience, there are elements of the evaluation and assessment process that introverts may, in their present form, have trouble with. Let's examine the potential for difficulty by first exploring some of the many methods that student affairs professionals use to evaluate student leaders.

Event Post-Mortems

Completed in the immediate aftermath of an event, program, or project, these quick gatherings are timed to collect first impressions on how a project was executed. These meetings are helpful when capturing small moments that could potentially be forgotten, or more immediate concerns that need to be dealt with presently.

Why They Work

Waiting to meet about events can allow for a "smoothing over" of reactions and feedback; when gathered in a more immediate fashion, opinions and observations are likely to carry more candor.

Why Introverts May Struggle

The nature of introverted thinking makes these quick responses difficult to come by. In the absence of time to reflect on the happenings that have recently transpired, you may get little more from an introvert than "I don't know," and s/he will be telling the truth!

Focus Groups

Helpful when gathering feedback not just from those with whom you regularly meet, focus groups bring a number of students (and other constituents, if desired) to collect their opinions and impressions on a topic or initiative. Ideas, recommendations, and concerns given in these forums are recorded, often informing programmatic design and improvement.

Why They Work
In a "survey overload" culture on campus, focus groups can be a refreshing opportunity to meet with students affected by the work we do, while gathering feedback and opinions that may not be able to be captured in the traditional survey format. Tone of responses is easier to discern than it can be in writing.

Why Introverts May Struggle
While introversion is by no means synonymous with shyness or anti-social tendencies, they can be ill at ease when asked to express opinions in group settings; this discomfort can be heightened in groups comprised of individuals they don't know.

Performance Reviews
Typically conducted at the end of a semester or year, performance reviews are a one-on-one meeting specifically designed to address the strengths and weaknesses of a term of service. They can be preceded by the opportunity for the reviewed to complete a self-evaluation, or can be conducted "cold," without the chance to collect thoughts or reflect beforehand. Depending on the desired outcome, either approach can be deemed correct.

Why They Work

One on one meetings may get cancelled and staff meetings don't always offer the chance to address issues of performance, but these periodic evaluations provide a dedicated opportunity. Performance reviews serve as an opportunity to reliably address concerns — or, for that matter, triumphs and successes — that may arise with an individual's performance. While these concerns can (and should!) be broached well in advance of these relatively infrequent meetings, it provides a convenient opportunity to address them in relation to one's overall success or challenge in a role.

Why Introverts May Struggle

In the absence of a chance to prep for these meetings, introverts may be at a loss when asked to thoughtfully answer the probing questions posed in this setting. Additionally, performance reviews often rely on the ability to convey thoughts and opinions verbally; this synchronous form of communication, while manageable, may not yield the most fully fleshed-out results.

Exit Interviews

Similar in tone to performance reviews, but reserved explicitly for the conclusion of an individual's term of service, exit interviews can help provide valuable information about how a role is structured, as well as how it was performed by the individual in it. Exit interviews have the potential to cover more ground than a performance review, particularly if a student's time in a role spans multiple terms.

Why They Work
Exit interviews give valuable insight not just on an individual's performance, but also on the structure of a role- balance of duties, reporting structure, additional resources needed, etc. As with performance reviews, day-to-day opportunities to look more holistically at a position often slip by in favor of more seemingly immediate concerns. Ensuring that time is dedicated to look at structural and performance based factors can be extraordinarily valuable to an organization.

Why Introverts May Struggle
Many of the concerns that apply to performance reviews (ability to eloquently encapsulate a long term of service) come into play with exit interviews, perhaps more so if the individual has served in the role for a long period. Additionally, longer neural pathways for introverts means specific concerns may take longer to recall and will require more energy to do so.

I point out potential struggles for introverts in each of the aforementioned scenarios not to dissuade you from using any of these strategies; on the contrary, I think there is tremendous value to each method. However, there are a few strategies that could allow you to yield more satisfying, usable, and robust responses from introverts if they do struggle in any of the previously listed scenarios.

Share questions in advance. Each of the aforementioned scenarios features an instance where questions are posed to individuals. Going into these scenarios cold will lessen the likelihood of dynamic and robust responses. Do you have standard questions that you ask in these interviews or meetings? Let all students (introverts and extroverts alike) know what will be asked of them, and encourage them to ponder their responses before their meetings or focus groups. Just as with any interview they'll likely participate in for employment or program acceptance, we want students to prepare; these evaluation opportunities are no exception. If you're not already sharing questions in advance, I'd encourage you to try it and see if it affects the nature of responses you receive.

Vary the medium of response. Asynchronous communication is less sensitive to overstimulation that can slow introverts down, because it innately provides time to think and respond. If you find that you're having a difficult time gleaning meaningful responses from any student to questions that come up in evaluation interviews, consider providing multiple venues for response. Some students will not have a hard time articulating their answers verbally, but others will come to life when allowed to share answers in writing, through annotated photographs, drawings, or short videos. If you expand the scope of response beyond speaking, it will not only expand your reach in terms of student communication style, but also break up the experience with multiple formats of response. Admittedly, evaluation and assessment is not always the most engaging process; a multimedia presentation of data keeps it interesting!

One way I've done this is by incorporating the popular card game Apples to Apples into my evaluation process.

Questions are still shared in advance, but rather than encouraging a student to answer in an open-ended fashion, I ask them to pick three "green" (Adjective cards) to express their response. That card selection was then followed by guiding questions about why each word was selected. For your reference, here's an example of the sorts of question I posed, and how I analyzed responses:

Pick a card to describe how supported you felt by fellow staff members.

Common Answers: efficient, beneficial
Notable Answers: isolated, lopsided

For this one, I made sure to ask separately about how staff members interacted (interpersonal), as well as how supported they felt by fellow staff (professional). In many cases, students expressed pleasure with the people that they worked with interpersonally, but some stress in the organization was revealed.

The two main problems that were revealed in this process was a feeling of isolation by our production team (who is scheduled separately and doesn't meet with our PR, programming or hospitality students), and a feeling of lopsidedness concerning motivation for work by staff members (who works because they like it, who works because they need a job, what does each version look like?)

As you'll see, this allowed for more descriptive responses than the standard "good" or "fine" answers that we so often hear in evaluation meetings.

Encourage narrative response. Storytelling is a natural impulse; the brain naturally seeks to make sense of our surroundings and experiences, and therefore seeks to organize information into a story structure. Even the slightest alteration of a question can feed this instinct; rather than asking "What did you feel like you were strong at this year?", consider posing the question, "Tell me about a time where you felt extremely competent this year. What were you doing? Who were you working with?" Both questions could yield similar responses, but the ease with which the latter can be answered is important to helping those who may have trouble in the selected evaluation format.

In addition to providing ways to tweak existing forms of evaluation, I also want to make a case for reflective practices such as journaling or blogging as a means of programmatic and positional assessment. As has been mentioned previously in this volume, the asynchronous nature of blogging is a boon to introverted students, and the opportunity to have a dedicated space to share thoughts can be invaluable to learning more about their take on experiences and processes. This can also provide much needed "practice in bravery" as they learn to package their thoughts in a manner suitable for public consumption- a benefit that should be noted for all students, not just introverts!

In addition to recognition that introverted students feel more at home expressing themselves in writing (and online), high school teacher Michelle Lampinen also shares that students' extroverted counterparts benefit from this form of reflection:

> Introverted students tend to share more online than they do in person; blogging is an invaluable way for me to get to know them better as people and students. It's also great to see reserved students garnering attention from their peers. Furthermore, students understand the importance of hearing many voices. One recently noted that she enjoys the blogs because **"[s]ome of the quieter folks during discussion can talk about their opinions too, so we finally get to hear them."** (emphasis added)

Whatever method you choose to evaluate students, know that working with an introvert should never by any means be used as an excuse to couch or lessen negative feedback. Honest evaluation is a gift to anyone who receives it; in its absence, the student may not be able to improve constructively. With that said, recognize that it may be difficult for the student to work through the criticism and advice given. When I coach fellow staff members on this topic, I provided tips on how to consider these moments when they occur. As you continue to work with these students, work with them to incorporate the following practices into their reflection:

Restore equilibrium. For all your efforts to temper your reaction to a disappointment or letdown, it may still take you a moment to return to equilibrium. Take that moment. Trying to suppress it or push it off will only place you further off balance, making you more uncomfortable. If you need to adjourn to the nearest restroom, your car, or some hidden place on campus, do so to regain your composure. There is nothing wrong with feeling an emotion fully; allow yourself to do so, with the aid of the other tips listed here.

Adopt a mantra. A mantra isn't going to fix the deep pain, frustration, embarrassment or shame that you feel in the moment after you're hurt, but it will help you to restore composure until you're in an environment where you can truly allow yourself to feel. This mantra should acknowledge what you're feeling, advise you to momentarily put the feeling away, and reassure you that you will overcome what troubles you. One of my go-to mantras to help divert my frustrations is: "This is uncomfortable right now. But you know it'll pass. You can do this." A series of short sentences, as simple as that, can keep you from the rare but significant outbursts introverts can have when overwhelmed.

Recall triumphs. Because introverts find it so easy to retreat to their own thoughts, they have long memories. But all humans, regardless of temperament, hold bad memories more tightly than good ones. The result, for introverts, can be a loop of bad experiences and disappointments. When you're feeling low or defeated, challenge yourself to recall the good memories. Chances are, you have had positive experiences as often (or more often!) as you've had bad ones. Find the good, and allow those moments to fill your thoughts. Don't discount the lessons that can be learned from your mistakes, but don't take the occurrence of a mistake to mean that you're incapable of success either.

Take to the paper. One of my favorite presidents, and a noted introvert, is Abraham Lincoln. Lincoln was a master of the unsent letter. In *Lincoln on Leadership*, Donald T. Phillips spoke of Lincoln's habit of venting frustration through "extended letters of refutation." Phillips noted that the act itself provided the necessary catharsis; "he felt better for having stated his case but did not want any of his angry or emotional remarks made public." A great gift of the introverted mind is its ability to brilliantly and vividly express itself in writing. In times of frustration, high anxiety, or sadness, carry these feelings to the page. Don't worry about grammar, convention, or wording- just express yourself. The ability to express your feelings without judgment or interruption will likely help you calm down, easing your return to equilibrium.

To return to the question voiced at the start of the chapter- evaluation and assessment meetings serve as an invaluable opportunity to help student leaders find out if they, as Perkis cruelly puts it, "have value." But it doesn't have to be the harrowing and intimidating experience that it can sometimes seem to be. By monitoring the nature of your process, varying the manner in which questions are asked and responded to, and helping students to work through the results, all students can feel confident and comfortable stepping onto the proverbial scale of their skills and abilities.

INsights: 5 Ways to Evaluate & Assess the Involvement and Leadership Experience of Introverts

1. **If an evaluation opportunity is on the horizon, ensure that the method of evaluation is shared in advance.** Provide a rubric early (even at the start of the term of service!), and provide any questions that will be posed to the student ahead of time.

2. **Recognize that spoken reflection is not the default/ most effective method for many introverts.** While some may be comfortable speaking their mind, others may prefer to "write" their mind, or "film" it. Prepare for this possibility, and encourage it if possible.

3. **Utilize prompts or interactive elements if needed.** By allowing memories to be jogged, either through momentary tools or previous reflections, more robust responses will likely follow. The rush of energy it takes to recall important responses in a critical period, can be lessened when something exists or is permitted to prime the proverbial pump.

4. **Share stories.** While one may not easily be able to answer the question "what have you learned," it may be easier to say "Tell me about a time in your tenure that [this] happened." Utilize the brain's affinity for narratives to simplify the response process, and also lessening the pressure by allowing the narrator to tell a story he or she already knows.

5. **Recognize that this is a difficult process, and help students work through negative feedback.** Without minimizing necessary moments of struggle, seek to assist in the internalization and learning that comes with making mistakes, or even failing outright. Through continuous check-ins, development of mantras, and

recognition of the misstep in context, these defeats don't have to be crushing ones.

With talk of bright spots, let's now move ahead to the final stage of the involvement and leadership process: acknowledging the good through recognition and rewards. But first, an interlude about how to create a positive environment for introverts to give and receive feedback.

INTERLUDE: PROVIDING CONSTRUCTIVE FEEDBACK FOR INTROVERTS
by Joel Pettigrew

In addition to providing the tools to help you work with introverted students to improve their performance, I'm pleased to present Joel's perspective on how to create an environment ripe for these conversations, as well as a few tips on how to approach an introvert who may need you as a sounding board.

One of the first things we tend to think of when considering introverts, whether in our personal or work life, is that they tend to be quiet more often than not. Most of the time, we are quietly observing, speaking when we are moved to, but also definitely have our louder "extroverted" times, just as our extroverted counterparts have their quieter moments.

As an introvert, particularly a quiet one with a terrible case of resting jerk face, whose extroverted moments revolve around craft beer and soccer, I know I'm a difficult employee and former student to advise. It takes a lot for me to open up, and even when conditions are right to do so, I find myself keeping my most intense feelings or thoughts in, because I've already thought way too much about how they'll be received (95% of the time, I figure it will go negatively).

Getting constructive feedback is not difficult, as I've probably already thought a lot about my work and what I've been doing and it's helpful to gain another perspective on what I've already obsessed over. It's the asking for feedback that is tough – most of the time. First and foremost, I think there has to be a lot of established trust in the relationship, because opening myself up to feedback (I am the only one allowed to be critical about myself) requires the other person to know me well. There also has to be a critical mass of emotion behind the ask, meaning either I've thought too much about the topic and am going in circles in my head, or that it is overwhelming – a decision too big to be made internally or an issue that needs to be addressed immediately. The thing with advising introverts is knowing that at some point, they will make the ask for constructive feedback on some major issue, because we know when we are ready to talk (remember the part about how we speak when we are moved to). A good advisor, supervisor, or mentor is open to the simultaneous randomness and importance of those moments. For me, they won't come up during weekly one on ones, because those are too 'on the spot' feeling, and they are more likely to be on schedule with how worked up I am about a particular issue.

Two stories, to illustrate that critical mass that necessitates the need for constructive, and real, feedback come from my grad school search and as a young professional.

Going to graduate school is (duh) a big decision. Trying to sync the decision up with a long-distance boyfriend who is searching for grad school in another field made the process even more stressful for me. Adding to the stress of the decision itself are the interview days, which are basically student affairs' way of telling me I should have gone to grad school in good old introverted history. Shuffling from interview to interview, trying to remember every person's name, listening to a new story every five minutes from fellow candidates, and then either sharing a room with a fellow candidate, or having to be hosted by a current cohort member was basically my nightmare, and likely the same for many introverts.

My first interview weekend was at Miami University of Ohio, my second overall choice, and with no context to place it in... I was hooked. I came back to homebase at Texas A&M completely confused, exhausted from the process, but excited about what I had seen without anything to compare it to. My advisor, with whom I had developed a deep relationship with over two years and various leadership positions, knew something was up and provided me the opportunity to make the ask. What followed was a one hour conversation, including tears, but that got me in the right headspace to approach the next two interview weekends with an open-mind and open eyes, and with a valuable context she was able to provide.

The key to advising introverts is knowing that at some point, you will need to clear your schedule and heart for them to make that ask of you, and during that conversation you must be real and honest. Tell them the necessary information they need to hear, and do not sugarcoat issues or decisions they need to consider. Sugarcoating to an introvert is an invitation for them to keep the conversation within their own head, and that is opposite of how you want to approach these conversations. Constructive and honest feedback during these moments is essential to the development of strong and forward-moving introverts, and should be expected with the amount of trust that gets built prior to the ask.

As a young professional, I still suffer from considering major decisions or thinking about important decisions without an appropriate context in which to place my thoughts. With only a few years of experience under my belt, I rely on my own feelings on my work, but also the validation or feedback I get from experienced professionals around me on a daily basis. Getting constructive feedback is key to establishing an accurate image of my development as a professional, both good and bad, and it goes hand in hand with a matter of trust with supervisors.

For the first couple of years in my latest position, I received really positive feedback at almost every one on one with my supervisor; I was rarely taken to task. I knew I was doing good work, but with so much positive feedback and very little constructive feedback around my weaknesses or areas for improvement, I developed an inaccurate image of myself in relation to my work with my supervisor. However, that streak came to a screeching halt, and I found myself leaving a couple one on ones in a row angry, frustrated, and confused by what I felt like was an onslaught of negative feedback, both deserved and undeserved. Stewing over that negative feedback for a couple of weeks, I had finally worked myself up enough to make the ask about why this sudden change in the feedback I was getting and what had necessitated it. Thankfully, my supervisor recognized how stressed and frustrated I was and set aside a good chunk of time to chat behind closed doors.

Explaining both our sides, we came to understand that my supervisor had not completely realized that she had kept me in a positive feedback loop for a long time, informing my own understanding of my work as a young professional. From this, I took constructive feedback more negatively than it was intended, had interpreted feedback on areas of growth as attacks, and had not fully understood areas where I truly was weak and needed to improve on quickly. I had to make the ask to balance a relationship which, in truth, had been uneven from the beginning, and my supervisor allowed time for me to parse out my thoughts and feelings that I had been stewing over for weeks. We came out with a better understanding of each of our sides of the advising relationship and with a reestablished trust in the process.

In the end, introverts thrive on trust, and though we may be content in our own heads more often than not, it is the feedback of valued friends and colleagues that help us truly understand who we are and if we are doing well in work and life. When all of the messiness gets overwhelming, the key to effectively supervising and providing growth opportunities for introverts is to be ready for the ask, and to welcome it with time, patience, and honesty. Your introverted supervisee will be better off for the time, care, and trust you have placed in them; you will have a better understanding of who they are, but also who they are to you- an essential piece in providing constructive feedback to introverts.

chapter 7

RECOGNITION & REWARDS

Did you know that a (nearly) full-sized adult can fit under the seat of a school bus?
I learned this from experience on August 23rd, 2006.

I wasn't hiding from danger, or embarrassment, or from bullying or teasing. I was hiding from a chorus, sing-screaming "The Birthday Song" at the top of their lungs. I was further startled and shaken by a head poking down next to mine, my friend Sami, to make sure I heard every word.

This isn't the first time that such recognition brought my insides to the brink of curdling. As it happens, it generally involves being sung to on my birthday. But I've also learned in the years since that this reaction to being pushed into the center of attention, is by no means uncommon for introverts. While many care deeply about being appreciated by the people around them, few will revel in the opportunity for that appreciation to be shown in a public forum. Sophia Dembling put it beautifully: ***"I accept attention, sometimes I invite it, but I don't compete for it."***

"Wait a minute," you may be wondering, "doesn't this vision of introverts reinforce some of the stereotypes ascribed to them?" In some ways, I suppose it does. To say "be careful how you recognize introverts! No surprises! Watch out!" makes them appear fragile, volatile even, like an unstable chemical compound or a jack-in-the-box. But the reason I'm so bullish about making this point is because a lack of care when doing so reinforces different stereotypes about introverts, ones that aren't so nice. The rush of "power usage" that comes from being unable to effectively manage the energy that an unexpected place in a ceremony, results in an appearance of standoffishness, indifference, or a lack of gratitude- persistent stereotypes and misconceptions that sadly already plague introverts.

At the same time, many of us survive in (and perhaps, whether meaning to or not, cultivate) an environment devoid of recognition. Seeking efficiency and efficacy, we overlook what it may mean to praise the good work of a colleague or advisee. While this move may seem easier on all, few (irrespective of temperament) thrive in this version of a work climate. To halt recognition because "there isn't time" or because it makes some people uncomfortable, isn't an effective solution either. We always have time for what we prioritize, and I'm of the belief that showing appreciation and recognition for good work should always be a priority.

Not only do I wish that the landscape of rewards and recognition were better for introverts, but I wish it were better overall. But we'll concentrate on the former here; I'll briefly share a few tips on how to recognize the good work and growth of introverted student leaders without sending them retreating to the safety of the underside of a seat. It's uncomfortable under there. I'll note that many of these tips apply to recognition in the form of ceremonies; after that, I'll share a few more private recognition and reward methods that could take the place of a large event.

Change the time of day. As odd as it may seem, it may make more sense to hold some of these recognition ceremonies early in the day. In addition to getting the work day off to a good start, the quieter of your students stand a chance of being better energized early in the day, before their daily routines and other elements have had the opportunity to wear on them. It presents different logistical challenges than a ceremony later in the day, but advance notice can sometimes address that concern.

Let them know in advance. Speaking of advance notice...a quick note to those that like awards to be a surprise: not everyone likes, or works well under, those conditions. And the rush of stimulation that comes with an attempt to simultaneously comprehend a surprise and a surprise space in the spotlight, is an excellent recipe for introvert overwhelm.

By the same token, I'm sensitive to the notion of wanting there to be some semblance of suspense to the proceedings. To that end, I would recommend informing honorees of a nomination, and strongly encouraging attendance. That combination allows individuals to prepare for the inevitability of taking the stage, and presents a bit of the mystique that is so attractive to those that do like surprises.

Enlist the help of those they've bonded with. As we've established elsewhere in this volume, introverts take personal bonds very seriously; they serve to ground them, provide a sense of stability in a world that can sometimes sneak up on you. Should you elect to maintain uncertainty or high stimulation in your proceedings, do your best to ensure that there is someone in the audience or nearby who they are comfortable with and can provide a calming presence amidst a scenario that may feel chaotic in the moment.

If your students are allowed to bring outside guests, encourage they bring a close family member or friend to the ceremony with them (another way of signifying, "Hey, something's going to happen!"); if space doesn't allow for it, encourage they have a friend or mentor from campus on hand.

Quietly spread the word. David Zweig, author of the book "Invisibles," expertly unpacked this term as a means to classify those who fit some or all of the following traits: generally ambivalent to recognition, meticulous, and comfortable taking on responsibility*. While invisibles are not all introverted (by any means), it is a common station that introverts find themselves in. They don't work or excel for recognition, but at the same time would like their good and hard work to be appreciated. A great way to do this is to share meaningfully news of awards and recognition.

Consider pairing an award with a press release to be sent to a student's hometown newspaper, a detailed LinkedIn recommendation or recommendation letter, or a note of gratitude to send to family members (one year, on Student Employee Appreciation Day, I crafted thank you notes to my two students, and mailed thank you notes to their parents). If your campus uses a news dissemination platform such as Merit, ensure that this accomplishment is verified on their profile, so it announces itself without them having to negotiate nervousness about "tooting their own horn."

Separate your spoons and glasses. Unless you know someone has prepared a speech (to this day, the only time I know of someone having a speech prepared for what was otherwise deemed a surprise, was my father at his 50th birthday party), don't ask that someone - anyone! - speak extemporaneously when receiving an award. Some of the reasons for this may be logistical, but others are temperamental. In *The Introvert's Way*, Sophia Dembling draws a connection between introversion and a common trait associated with them, preparedness: "Introverts think carefully before they speak. We can be excellent public speakers because we prepare carefully."* As such, a request for an eloquent speech within moments of winning may be infeasible. Think, after all, of actors and actresses who ascend the stage at the Oscars. Those who don't prepare speeches rarely knock it out of the park- this could be part of the reason why.

Save it for posterity. How can a few hours of recognition be meaningfully recalled in the years ahead? A hint: it will likely take more than a small bundle of candy or a votive candle. It's always nice to have something to refer back to as motivation during your tougher seasons; not a souvenir, but something more substantive. Could you allow winners to keep copies of the speeches given at their acceptance? Do you share the nomination letters with them? Is the ceremony recorded? Any of these methods could be used as an additional gift for those who win. To be able to take in the pride and accomplishment of the moment in one's own time is among the greatest gifts you could give an introvert (or anyone, for that matter!); finding a way to do so would be a wonderful way of acknowledging your appreciation for them.

As I mentioned, these tips largely apply in reference to award ceremonies, only one method of recognition you could choose to employ. I want to close this short chapter by sharing a few guidelines for recognition overall, inspired by talent scholar Meghan Biro's philosophy of how to structure these everyday interactions:

Recognize individuals in the moment.
If someone does something exceptional (please note: not just good), and they merit praise, there's no need to wait to give it to them. Tell them they did well, that their contribution or act was appreciated. Many don't need to hear much more than that.

Recognize individuals in context.

This means resisting the urge to save your praise for performance reviews, and it really means not just waiting until they seem to need the pick-me-up. Recognition given in context feels authentic, when done so out of context is jarring at best, and difficult to believe in at worst.

Craft recognition that is appropriate in volume or scale.
As Biro puts it, "recognition should match effort and results, or it loses meaning." Sending someone an Edible Arrangement because they cover for you when you're late to a meeting is a sweet gesture (at times literally), but doesn't quite fit the level of effort or investment expended (unless it's a huge meeting). Flashy shows of appreciation often aren't needed; if helpful, think to yourself "how would this person like to be thanked?"

Craft recognition that is authentic, not automatic.
As you may divine from the length of this section in comparison to others, this is an important one to me. If you don't have anything nice to say...don't fake it or everyone will know. False praise can, at times, feel worse than actual praise- why doesn't this person appreciate me or my work enough to understand why it's good? Nearly two years ago, I wrote on this very topic, urging that we give praise as specific as when we are asked to provide criticism:

> There's nothing in the world wrong with wanting someone to notice and acknowledge when you're working hard, doing good things, and accomplishing goals. A culture that awkwardly straddles modesty and self-promotion has trained us to shrug off these compliments when they come, and it has led to

seeming needy when wanting someone to notice you or your work. But this need is not wrong. Working solely based on this need, working exclusively for extrinsic motivation, is a different affair; the same can be said for wanting praise for doing what is base for your position or role. But the wish for acknowledgement of good work is not a moral failing or emotional weakness. [...]

But being able to praise good work is an incomplete request. In a week where circumstance and workload combined to leave me exhausted, resentful, and with a feeling of being left to twist in the wind unsupported, I couldn't understand why the kind words of friends and colleagues weren't making me feel any better. Please note, it is not to diminish the sentiment behind those words- I appreciate everyone who took time to lift me up at a time I couldn't do so for myself, you have no idea how much I needed to read or hear those words. But there was something missing still, and Francesca Catalano's words helped me discover why*:

In my job, I've allowed vulnerability to drive actions and have been turned down or just plain dismissed. Additionally, many of the times I've received positive feedback, it's been very general and overall unhelpful. More of a "Way to go, slugger! You're a star!" than anything I find useful, no matter how hard I insist on specific comments on my work. Usually, I get this vague style of feedback when it seems like I'm desperate for some kind of validation, and so I've kind of conditioned myself to resent compliments. [emphasis added]

Francesca makes a key observation that distinguishes praise from good praise. And I thank her for making it, because I couldn't figure out why I was feeling so hollow even as students would say "thank you" or my boss would say "Good work". Just as we push ourselves to be specific when giving negative feedback (after all, if we're general here, nothing will improve!), we should be equally specific when giving praise. Aimless and nonspecific platitudes, particularly in relationships where specificity can be reasonably expected (supervisor/supervisee, mentor/mentee, student employee, etc.), aren't helpful.

Inauthentic or nonspecific praise can have diminishing returns- both in your perception from students or supervisees, and in the quality of their work, if others suspect that the true nature and ardor of their work is being overlooked; if I had to elevate one tip provided here over all others, this would be the one.

Tie recognition to what an employee sees as valuable. For many involved students and student leaders, money can't serve as an incentive the way it would for some employees. What do your students want from their experience? Free food? Credits? Recommendations? Chipotle gift cards? Pay attention to the students that you work with closely enough, to know what they would value in their praise...and then act on that information. As an example, I've been given cookies as a thank you, but can't eat gluten, so this form of recognition was well-placed but ultimately not valuable for me.

We've been conditioned to think that recognition and rewards should come at the end of something- the end of a year, semester, or project. But infusing it into daily operations for all students (again, irrespective of temperament) can make a world of difference in keeping your team motivated, productive, and gracious toward one another.

INsights: 5 Ways to Recognize & Reward The Leadership and Involvement of Introverts

1. **Public spectacles not required.** For introverts, who are accustomed to (And in some cases, prefer!) staying out of the spotlight, recognition doesn't have to put them center stage. Consider ways to recognize the good work and accomplishments of introverts, without making them feel exposed or overly vulnerable.

2. **Resist the urge to shut down altogether.** Not knowing how to recognize someone, isn't a good excuse for not doing so. Take the opportunity to ask what makes them feel most appreciated, and seek to reward them in that fashion. The effort to not just honor their good work, but honor it in a way that makes them feel good, will be greatly appreciated.

3. **Seek to include loved ones.** When in situations of high stimulation, such as those that may overwhelm, it can be helpful to have friends and family who understand us

best at our side. If possible, find ways to provide connections to these trusted confidants to lessen the overwhelm that can come with these appreciated but energy-sapping moments.

4. **Make it meaningful.** Praise is best received when it is specific, timely, and genuine. Craft this sort of praise by giving it in the moment, noticing and citing details, and making it appropriate for the action its directed toward.

5. **Help it last.** Even after a seemingly interminable moment of being overstimulated passes, it is always nice for the product of the praise to last. Taping ceremonies, sharing nomination letters, or providing copies of speeches are all excellent examples of this.

conclusion

"I tend to shy away from books that focus on helping [a child] to 'overcome' being an introvert. Although I think it's important to help children learn to effectively navigate our extrovert-dominated world, I don't see introversion as a characteristic that needs to be 'overcome,' and neither do psychologists."
-Mark Phillips, "Introversion and the Invisible Adolescent

Well, we've arrived at the end. From recruitment to rewards, we've examined ways to make the introverted involvement and leadership experience easier and less draining. I hope you don't feel as though the journey was designed to "treat" introversion or wish it away. Rather, it is hoped that you've seen how elements of these processes that feel so natural in their current state could be adapted or reconsidered to thoughtfully include the introverted personality *without* leaving extroverts to be disadvantaged. When I think about the moments I felt the most drained (after a long day of training, asleep at the airport after a long and crowded conference, at a loss for words in my end-of-the year review), the memories drive me to quietly but openly assist introverted students as they move through similar experiences with a greater awareness of how they're feeling…and why.

I want very badly to help you execute the tips in this book, as well as any others that you may want to try out on students in need. Please feel free to keep in touch via http://www.ammamarfo.com/lightitupbook, and let me know how you (and your students) are doing! I would truly love to help however I can.

references

PREFACE

The Grant, Gino and Hoffman study referenced, "Reversing the Extraverted Leadership Advantage: The Role of Employer Proactivity" was completed in 2011 and first appeared in *The Academy of Management Journal.*

Astin's seminal 1984 study outlining his theory on student involvement was published under the name "Student Involvement: A Developmental Theory for Higher Education" in the *Journal of College Student Development.*

The I's Have It: Reflections on Introversion in Student Affairs is my first book about the interplay of introversion and its role in higher education. It is referred to several times over the course of this book, and is available for purchase at http://www.ammamarfo.com/book.

Astin's follow-up to his student development theory was outlined in a Q&A for ACUI's *Bulletin* in 2012.

INTRODUCTION

A League of their Own was released in 1992 by Columbia Pictures.

Adam Grant's 2014 demystification of introversion first appeared in *Psychology Today* as "5 Myths About Introverts and Extraverts at Work," and was re-published through Susan Cain's Quiet Revolution under the same name.

Genius of Opposites by Jennifer Kahnweiler was released in August 2015 by Berrett-Koehler Publishers.

CHAPTER 3

Nicole Onofreo's 2014 paper was entitled "Examining the Effectiveness of Student Involvement Recruitment Strategies for Introverts."

CHAPTER 4

Sophia Dembling's book is entitled *The Introvert Way: Living a Quiet Life in a Noisy World,* and was released in 2012 by Perigee Books.

Laura McClernon's book is entitled *Stop Repeating, Start Recording*, and was released in 2014 via Kindle Direct Publishing.

The 2002 Judge, Bono, and Iles study was referenced in Grant, Gino, and Hoffman's aforementioned piece (see the Preface).

Bergman and Sams built a five-piece flipped classroom toolkit featured on *Edutopia* in 2014.

Guy Chmieleski authored a 2012 article titled "Unlikeky Student Leaders (?) - The Introverts" with *Faith on Campus*.

Randy Brown detailed his flipped classroom strategy in an article entitled "Flipping the Unflippable Classes" on *Edutopia* in 2014.

CHAPTER 5

Susan Cain has a periodic advice series on her Quiet Revolution website where she elaborated on the difference between shyness and introversion.

Dunkel and Schuh released *Advising Student Groups and Organizations* in 1997 with Jossey-Bass Publishers.

Several studies mentioned here were revealed through Grant, Gino, and Hoffman's 2011 study on introversion and leadership in the workplace (see Preface).

Simon Sinek released *Start with Why* in 2011 with Portfolio Publishers.

Kahnweiler released *Quiet Influence: The Introvert's Guide to Making a Difference* in 2013 with Berrett-Koehler Publishers.

CHAPTER 6

Heavyweights was released in 1995 through Walt Disney Pictures.

Michelle Lampinen blogged about the role that writing and reflection has in her classroom via Edutopia in 2013 in a piece entitled "Blogging in the 21st Century Classroom."

Donald T. Phillips released Lincoln on Leadership: Executive Strategies for Tough Times in 2013 with DTP/Companion Books.

CHAPTER 7

David Zweig released *Invisibles: The Power of Anonymous Work in an Age of Relentless Self-Promotion* in 2014 with Portfolio Publishers.

Meghan Biro authored the 2013 *Forbes* article entitled "5 Ways Leaders Rock Employee Recognition."

acknowledgments

With little exception, I am blessed to have many of the same people in my corner as I complete this book, as I did when I embarked on this journey the first time around. I will attempt to list them in no particular order (I'm serious, so please no offense at where you're placed!):

Sue Caulfield, Joel Pettigrew, Jeff Parker, Curtis Tarver, Jason Meier, Valerie Heruska, Laura McClernon, Rose Rezaei, Nicole Onofreo, Aly Keves, Chris Conzen, Joe Ginese, Mallory Bower, Jana Lithgow, Paromita De, Meg Ward, Steven Harowitz, Teri Bump, Nancy Hunter Denney, the Lonardos Mike and Andy, and Mike Zakarian.

To all my friends and family who endured me saying "I had plans" and wrote...and acknowledged that writing does actually count as plans.

To the students I've worked with over the past several years that showed me how relevant this work is.

To the professionals and students who have consumed this information through conferences, blogs, workshops, and the peppering of questions- this wouldn't have happened without you.

To the fellow introversion writers who have been gracious enough to respond to inquiries, send encouragement, and provide resources (knowingly or otherwise) that informed my writing: Susan Cain, Sophia Dembling, Adam Grant, Jennifer Kahnweiler, Joshua Wolf Shenk, David Zweig, and Laurie Helgoe.

And to my family, who continues to indulge the creative bookworm that once confidently claimed to write Shel Silverstein's *The Giving Tree*. This book won't top that, but I still feel good about it :)

www.ingramcontent.com/pod-product-compliance
Lightning Source LLC
Chambersburg PA
CBHW071123090426
42736CB00012B/1989